# CONFIGURATION MANAGEMENT
## Expert Guidance for Service Managers and Practiti

**BCS THE CHARTERED INSTITUTE FOR IT**

Our mission as BCS, The Chartered Institute for IT, is to enable the information society. We promote wider social and economic progress through the advancement of information technology, science and practice. We bring together industry, academics, practitioners and government to share knowledge, promote new thinking, inform the design of new curricula, shape public policy and inform the public.

Our vision is to be a world-class organisation for IT. Our 70,000 strong membership includes practitioners, businesses, academics and students in the UK and internationally. We deliver a range of professional development tools for practitioners and employees. As a leading IT qualification body, we offer a range of widely recognised qualifications.

**Further Information**
BCS The Chartered Institute for IT,
First Floor, Block D,
North Star House, North Star Avenue,
Swindon, SN2 1FA, United Kingdom.
T +44 (0) 1793 417 424
F +44 (0) 1793 417 444
**www.bcs.org/contactus**

# CONFIGURATION MANAGEMENT
## Expert Guidance for Service Managers and Practitioners

David Norfolk and Shirley Lacy

Published by British Informatics Society Limited (BISL), a wholly owned subsidiary of BCS The Chartered Institute for IT First Floor, Block D, North Star House, North Star Avenue, Swindon, SN2 1FA, UK. www.bcs.org

ISBN 978-1-906124-58-8

British Cataloguing in Publication Data.
A CIP catalogue record for this book is available at the British Library.

Typeset by Lapiz Digital Services, Chennai, India.
Printed at CPI Antony Rowe Ltd, Chippenham, UK.

# CONTENTS

# FIGURES AND TABLES

# AUTHORS

**Shirley Lacy** is Managing Director of ConnectSphere and specialises in the application of service management best practices to deliver value from IT investments. She leads ConnectSphere's assessment and IT service management practice group.

Shirley is highly regarded within the industry and is an authority on service management and configuration management practices. Shirley is a co-author of the OGC's ITIL Service Transition book with Ivor Macfarlane and the British Standards Institute (BSI) publications on Achieving ISO/IEC 20000 with Jenny Dugmore.

Shirley is the BCS, The Chartered Institute of IT representative on the British Standards committee for IT Service Management, IST/15/-8 BSI IT Service Management group (ISO/IEC 20000). She is the UK Principal Expert on the ISO Working Group for Process Assessment standards for software, systems and service management.

**David Norfolk** first got involved with enterprise systems computing professionally in 1978, and has worked in England and Australia in Database Administration; Development Method and Standards; Internal Control; Network Management; Operations Research; and even PC Support.

Working conditions in banking in the City in the 1990s eventually drove him into a career as an independent analyst and journalist. He has written for most of the news-stand PC and computing magazines in the UK as well as some in the Middle East and America, and is now an industry analyst with Bloor Research.

# ABBREVIATIONS

| | |
|---|---|
| **API** | Application Programming Interface |
| **BRM** | Business Relationship Management/Manager |
| **BSI** | The British Standards Institute |
| **CCO** | Chief Compliance Officer |
| **CCRM** | Change, Configuration and Release Management Specialist Group (itSMF) |
| **CFO** | Chief Financial Officer |
| **CI** | Configuration Item |
| **CIO** | Chief Information Officer |
| **CKO** | Chief Knowledge Officer |
| **CMDB** | Configuration Management Database |
| **CMM** | Capability Maturity Model |
| **CMMI®** | Capability Maturity Model Integration |
| **CMS** | Configuration Management System |
| **CMSG** | Configuration Management Specialist Group |
| **COBIT®** | Control Objectives for Information and related Technology |
| **COTS** | Commercial Off-The-Shelf |
| **CRO** | Corporate Risk Officer |
| **CSF** | Critical Success Factors |
| **CSI** | Continual Service Improvement |
| **DML** | Definitive Media Library |
| **DTAP** | Development, Testing, Acceptance and Production |
| **GUI** | Graphical User Interface |
| **IDE** | Integrated Development Environment |
| **IP** | Internet Protocol |

| | |
|---|---|
| **IEC** | International Electrotechnical Commission |
| **ISO** | International Organization for Standardization |
| **IT** | Information Technology |
| **ITSM** | IT Service Management |
| **itSMF** | IT Service Management Forum |
| **KPI** | Key Performance Indicator |
| **MTRS** | Mean Time to Restore Service |
| **OLA** | Operational Level Agreement |
| **PIR** | Post-Implementation Review |
| **PTM** | Physical Technology Model |
| **QM** | Quality Manager |
| **RFI** | Request For Information |
| **ROI** | Return On Investment |
| **RUP** | Rational Unified Process |
| **SACM** | Service Asset and Configuration Management |
| **SKMS** | Service Knowledge Management System |
| **SLA** | Service Level Agreement |
| **SLM** | Service Level Management/Manager |
| **SMART** | Specific, Measurable, Agreed, Realistic and Time-specific |
| **SMT** | Senior Management Team |
| **SOX** | Sarbanes–Oxley |
| **SVP** | Senior Vice President |
| **VP** | Vice President |

# GLOSSARY†

**Asset Management** (Service Transition) Asset Management is the Process responsible for tracking and reporting the value and ownership of financial Assets throughout their Lifecycle. Asset Management is part of an overall Service Asset and Configuration Management Process. See Asset Register.

**Asset Register** (Service Transition) A list of Assets, which includes their ownership and value. The Asset Register is maintained by Asset Management.

**Baseline** (Continual Service Improvement) A Benchmark used as a reference point. For example:

- An ITSM Baseline can be used as a starting point to measure the effect of a Service Improvement Plan.

- A Performance Baseline can be used to measure changes in Performance over the lifetime of an IT Service.

- A Configuration Management Baseline can be used to enable the IT Infrastructure to be restored to a known Configuration if a Change or Release fails.

**Build** (Service Transition) The Activity of assembling a number of Configuration Items to create part of an IT Service. The term Build is also used to refer to a Release that is authorised for distribution. For example Server Build or laptop Build.

**Capability Maturity Model (CMM)** (Continual Service Improvement) The Capability Maturity Model for Software (also known as the CMM and SW-CMM) is a model used to identify Best Practices to help increase Process Maturity. CMM was developed at the Software Engineering Institute (SEI) of Carnegie Mellon University. In 2000, the SW-CMM was upgraded to Capability Maturity Model Integration (CMMI®). The SEI no longer maintains the SW-CMM model, its associated appraisal methods, or training materials.

**Capability Maturity Model Integration (CMMI®)** (Continual Service Improvement) Capability Maturity Model Integration (CMMI®) is a process improvement approach developed by the Software Engineering Institute (SEI) of Carnegie Melon University. CMMI® provides organisations with the essential elements of effective processes. It can be used to guide process improvement across a project, a division, or an entire organisation. CMMI® helps integrate traditionally separate organisational functions, set process improvement goals and priorities, provide guidance for quality processes, and provide a point of reference for appraising current processes. See http://www.sei.cmu.edu/cmmi/ for more information.

**Change Management**   (Service Transition) The Process responsible for controlling the Lifecycle of all Changes. The primary objective of Change Management is to enable beneficial Changes to be made, with minimum disruption to IT Services.

**CI Type**   (Service Transition) A Category that is used to Classify CIs. The CI Type identifies the required Attributes and Relationships for a Configuration Record. Common CI Types include: hardware, Document, User etc.

**COBIT®**   (Continual Service Improvement) Control Objectives for Information and related Technology (COBIT®) provides guidance and Best Practice for the management of IT Processes. COBIT® is published by the IT Governance Institute. See http://www.isaca.org/ for more information.

**Configuration Baseline**   (Service Transition) A Baseline of a Configuration that has been formally agreed and is managed through the Change Management process. A Configuration Baseline is used as a basis for future Builds, Releases and Changes.

**Configuration Control**   (Service Transition) The Activity responsible for ensuring that adding, modifying or removing a CI is properly managed, for example by submitting a Request for Change or Service Request.

**Configuration Item (CI)**   (Service Transition) Any Component that needs to be managed in order to deliver an IT Service. Information about each CI is recorded in a Configuration Record within the Configuration Management System and is maintained throughout its Lifecycle by Configuration Management. CIs are under the control of Change Management. CIs typically include IT Services, hardware, software, buildings, people, and formal documentation such as Process documentation and SLAs.

**Configuration Management**   (Service Transition) The Process responsible for maintaining information about Configuration Items required to deliver an IT Service, including their Relationships. This information is managed throughout the Lifecycle of the CI. Configuration Management is part of an overall Service Asset and Configuration Management Process.

**Configuration Management Database (CMDB)**   (Service Transition) A database used to store Configuration Records throughout their Lifecycle. The Configuration Management System maintains one or more CMDBs, and each CMDB stores Attributes of CIs, and Relationships with other CIs.

**Configuration Management System (CMS)**   (Service Transition) A set of tools and databases that are used to manage an IT Service Provider's Configuration data. The CMS also includes information about Incidents,

Problems, Known Errors, Changes and Releases; and may contain data about employees, Suppliers, locations, Business Units, Customers and Users. The CMS includes tools for collecting, storing, managing, updating, and presenting data about all Configuration Items and their Relationships. The CMS is maintained by Configuration Management and is used by all IT Service Management Processes. See Configuration Management Database, Service Knowledge Management System.

**Critical Success Factor (CSF)**   Something that must happen if a Process, Project, Plan, or IT Service is to succeed. KPIs are used to measure the achievement of each CSF. For example a CSF of 'protect IT Services when making Changes' could be measured by KPIs such as 'percentage reduction of unsuccessful Changes', 'percentage reduction in Changes causing Incidents' etc.

**Definitive Media Library (DML)**   (Service Transition) One or more locations in which the definitive and approved versions of all software Configuration Items are securely stored. The DML may also contain associated CIs such as licences and documentation. The DML is a single logical storage area even if there are multiple locations. All software in the DML is under the control of Change and Release Management and is recorded in the Configuration Management System. Only software from the DML is acceptable for use in a Release.

**Gap Analysis**   (Continual Service Improvement) An Activity which compares two sets of data and identifies the differences. Gap Analysis is commonly used to compare a set of Requirements with actual delivery. See Benchmarking.

**International Organization for Standardization (ISO)**   The International Organization for Standardization (ISO) is the world's largest developer of Standards. ISO is a non-governmental organisation which is a network of the national standards institutes of 156 countries. Further information about ISO is available from http://www.iso.org/

**International Standards Organisation**   See International Organization for Standardization (ISO).

**ISO/IEC 20000**   ISO Specification and Code of Practice for IT Service Management. ISO/IEC 20000 is aligned with ITIL Best Practice.

**IT Service Management (ITSM)**   The implementation and management of Quality IT Services that meet the needs of the Business. IT Service Management is performed by IT Service Providers through an appropriate mix of people, Process and Information Technology. See Service Management.

**IT Service Management Forum (itSMF)**   The IT Service Management Forum is an independent Organisation dedicated to promoting a professional approach to IT Service Management. The itSMF is a not-for-profit membership organisation with representation in many countries around the world (itSMF Chapters). The itSMF and its membership contribute to the development of ITIL and associated IT Service Management Standards. See http://www.itsmf.com/ for more information.

**ITIL**   A set of Best Practice guidance for IT Service Management. ITIL is owned by the OGC and consists of a series of publications giving guidance on the provision of Quality IT Services, and on the Processes and facilities needed to support them. See http://www.itil.co.uk/ for more information.

**Key Performance Indicator (KPI)**   (Continual Service Improvement) A Metric that is used to help manage a Process, IT Service or Activity. Many Metrics may be measured, but only the most important of these are defined as KPIs and used to actively manage and report on the Process, IT Service or Activity. KPIs should be selected to ensure that Efficiency, Effectiveness, and Cost Effectiveness are all managed.

**Maturity**   (Continual Service Improvement) A measure of the Reliability, Efficiency and Effectiveness of a Process, Function, Organisation etc. The most mature Processes and Functions are formally aligned to Business Objectives and Strategy, and are supported by a framework for continual improvement.

**Maturity Level**   A named level in a Maturity model such as the Carnegie Mellon Capability Maturity Model Integration.

**Monitor Control Loop**   (Service Operation) Monitoring the output of a Task, Process, IT Service or Configuration Item; comparing this output with a predefined norm; and taking appropriate action based on this comparison.

**Office of Government Commerce (OGC)**   OGC owns the ITIL brand (copyright and trademark). OGC is a UK Government department that supports the delivery of the government's procurement agenda through its work in collaborative procurement and in raising levels of procurement skills and capability with departments. It also provides support for complex public sector projects.

**Operational Level Agreement (OLA)**   (Service Design) (Continual Service Improvement) An Agreement between an IT Service Provider and another part of the same organisation. An OLA supports the IT Service Provider's delivery of IT Services to Customers. The OLA defines the goods or Services to be provided and the responsibilities of both parties. For example there could be an OLA:

- between the IT Service Provider and a procurement department to obtain hardware in agreed times;
- between the Service Desk and a Support Group to provide Incident Resolution in agreed times.

**Post-Implementation Review (PIR)**   A Review that takes place after a Change or a Project has been implemented. A PIR determines if the Change or Project was successful, and identifies opportunities for improvement.

**Process Owner**   A Role responsible for ensuring that a Process is Fit for Purpose. The Process Owner's responsibilities include sponsorship, Design, Change Management and continual improvement of the Process and its Metrics. This Role is often assigned to the same person who carries out the Process Manager Role, but the two Roles may be separate in larger organisations.

**Release and Deployment Management**   (Service Transition) The Process responsible for both Release Management and Deployment.

**Release Management**   (Service Transition) The Process responsible for Planning, scheduling and controlling the movement of Releases to Test and Live Environments. The primary Objective of Release Management is to ensure that the integrity of the Live Environment is protected and that the correct Components are released. Release Management is part of the Release and Deployment Management Process.

**Release Process**   The name used by ISO/IEC 20000 for the Process group that includes Release Management. This group does not include any other Processes. Release Process is also used as a synonym for Release Management Process.

**Scope**   The boundary, or extent, to which a Process, Procedure, Certification, Contract etc. applies. For example the Scope of Change Management may include all Live IT Services and related Configuration Items, the Scope of an ISO/IEC 20000 Certificate may include all IT Services delivered out of a named data centre.

**Service Asset and Configuration Management (SACM)**   (Service Transition) The Process responsible for both Configuration Management and Asset Management.

**Service Catalogue**   (Service Design) A database or structured Document with information about all Live IT Services, including those available for Deployment. The Service Catalogue is the only part of the Service Portfolio published to Customers, and is used to support the sale and delivery of IT Services. The Service Catalogue includes information about deliverables, prices, contact points, ordering and request Processes.

**Service Design**   (Service Design) A stage in the Lifecycle of an IT Service. Service Design includes a number of Processes and Functions and is the title of one of the Core ITIL publications.

**Service Knowledge Management System (SKMS)**   (Service Transition) A set of tools and databases that are used to manage knowledge and information. The SKMS includes the Configuration Management System, as well as other tools and databases. The SKMS stores, manages, updates, and presents all information that an IT Service Provider needs to manage the full Lifecycle of IT Services.

**Service Level**   Measured and reported achievement against one or more Service Level Targets. The term Service Level is sometimes used informally to mean Service Level Target.

**Service Level Agreement (SLA)** (Service Design) (Continual Service Improvement) An Agreement between an IT Service Provider and a Customer. The SLA describes the IT Service, documents Service Level Targets, and specifies the responsibilities of the IT Service Provider and the Customer. A single SLA may cover multiple IT Services or multiple Customers.

**Service Manager** A manager who is responsible for managing the end-to-end Lifecycle of one or more IT Services. The term Service Manager is also used to mean any manager within the IT Service Provider. Most commonly used to refer to a Business Relationship Manager, a Process Manager, an Account Manager or a senior manager with responsibility for IT Services overall.

**Service Owner** (Continual Service Improvement) A Role which is accountable for the delivery of a specific IT Service.

**Service Strategy** (Service Strategy) The title of one of the Core ITIL publications. Service Strategy establishes an overall Strategy for IT Services and for IT Service Management.

**Service Transition** (Service Transition) A stage in the Lifecycle of an IT Service. Service Transition includes a number of Processes and Functions and is the title of one of the Core ITIL publications.

**Stakeholder** All people who have an interest in an Organisation, Project, IT Service etc. Stakeholders may be interested in the Activities, targets, Resources or Deliverables. Stakeholders may include Customers, Partners, employees, shareholders, owners etc.

**Tension Metrics** (Continual Service Improvement) A set of related Metrics, in which improvements to one Metric have a negative effect on another. Tension Metrics are designed to ensure that an appropriate balance is achieved.

**Transition** (Service Transition) A change in state, corresponding to a movement of an IT Service or other Configuration Item from one Lifecycle status to the next.

**Use Case** (Service Design) A technique used to define required functionality and Objectives, and to Design Tests. Use Cases define realistic scenarios that describe interactions between Users and an IT Service or other System.

**Version** (Service Transition) A Version is used to identify a specific Baseline of a Configuration Item. Versions typically use a naming convention that enables the sequence or date of each Baseline to be identified. For example Payroll Application Version 3 contains updated functionality from Version 2.

# USEFUL WEBSITES

www.bcs.org — BCS The Chartered Institute for IT

www.bcs-cmsg.org.uk — BCS Configuration Management Specialist Group

www.itil-officialsite.com/home/home.asp — ITIL®

www.itsmf.co.uk — IT Service Management Forum

# FOREWORD

The Configuration Management Specialist Group (CMSG – www.bcs-cmsg.org.uk/) of BCS The Chartered Institute for IT (www.bcs.org) was set up in 1995 to provide a forum for developing and promoting configuration management, as a discrete management process. This publication is the CMSG's contribution to providing a compact, practically based, vendor-independent, 'good practice' guide to making a configuration management system work in the real world.

The CMSG facilitates the free and open exchange of ideas, experience and best practice at regular workshops and special events. Its aims and objectives are to:

- establish a professional development scheme, plotting a career path for professionals in configuration, change and release management;
- influence training and education within the field to achieve professional standards;
- establish a code of practice and standards for configuration, change and release management professionals including formal accreditation;
- facilitate the free and open exchange of configuration, change and release management experiences and ideas;
- influence the production and content of national, European and international standards related to configuration, change and release management;
- promote the benefit of configuration, change and release management within the industry at large;
- assure that industry receives benefits to business from configuration, change and release management;
- guide the makers of software tools to support the work of configuration, change and release management.

In 2008, the CMSG joined forces with the UK branch of the itSMF (the IT Service Management Forum – www.itsmf.co.uk/) to present a conference entitled *The CMDB and CMS: The Powerhouse of Service Management* at the Olympia Conference Centre, London (8 & 9 July 2008).

This conference series is the premier UK event on change, release and configuration management for the ITIL® framework (www.itil-officialsite.com/home/home.asp) and ALM (Application Lifecycle Management). It represents an important milestone in the integration of conventional IT systems development and IT operations support as 'automated business service delivery', with the collaboration of the major user organisations in the field.

Presentations at the 2008 conference came from world leaders in the configuration management field, representing both practitioners and vendors, and included several people involved in the formulation of the ITIL v3 framework (from now on, unless we need to distinguish ITIL v3 from v2, this will just be referred to as 'ITIL') and associated standards. The conference objective was to both present existing knowledge concerning the way successful organisations are implementing their Configuration Management Database (CMDB)/Configuration Management System (CMS), and to capture new knowledge in this area from peer interactions between managers and practitioners working across the service lifecycle, in an open forum.

A novel aspect of this conference was a stream of 'interactive session' workshops using decision support tools that promote dynamic interaction, rich brainstorming and better discussion between users, practitioners and the vendor community. The knowledge gained from the workshops helped to create a shared understanding of today's challenges and the strategies that will cope with them as we move forward into a 'service-oriented' future. This understanding is presented in the present publication and the decision-support technology used is described towards the end of Chapter 1 (see Knowledge capture during the interactive sessions on page 4).


## AUDIENCE

This book is primarily directed towards practitioners in configuration management. However, the customers of configuration management, the service desk and operations teams, compliance and risk managers, service delivery managers and operations managers, and service managers and process owners are also considered to be important members of our target audience.

Vendors of configuration management technology are included in our audience and one conference objective was to have a shared understanding of the implementation issues with vendors (this was the theme of the last session in the plenary room). Effective vendors need to form long-term partnerships with practitioners and, thus, to understand their point of view. Technology is an essential part of the configuration management message, and the practical tips in this book and the people/process context it recommends, will ensure that the technology is seen to be successful in practice.

The reader value from this book is from the access it provides to sound practical knowledge from experienced practitioners in configuration management. In addition, the techniques and technology used to mine conference attendees' knowledge should be of interest both to vendors and their larger customers because it could be applied to their own conferences and seminars.

## CONTEXT

The relevant parts of ITIL have become the de facto standard for configuration management. This does not mean that everyone has adopted ITIL, or that they should do so, but that its definitions provide a convenient and widely available frame of reference for this publication.

Nevertheless, there are many standards and frameworks that require configuration management besides ITIL, including COBIT®, ISO/IEC 20000, ISO/IEC 27001 and CMMI®, as well as the more specific ISO 10007:2003 *Quality management systems – Guidelines for configuration management*, and ISO/IEC 19770-1:2006 *Information technology – Software asset management Part 1, Processes*, and the general standards for software and system lifecycle management, ISO/IEC 12207 and ISO/IEC 15288. In general, practitioners in these areas will find that there are accepted mappings onto ITIL. Many of the concepts and practices in ITIL are common to all of these standards and frameworks.

In ITIL, the overall objective for service management is to provide services to business customers that are fit for purpose, stable and reliable. Adopting the guidance enables a service provider to adapt its services and respond effectively as business demand changes with business need.

The *ITIL Service Transition* publication (ISBN 978-0-113310-48-7) provides guidance for the development and improvement of capabilities for transitioning new and changed services into live service operation including change management, configuration management, asset management, release management and deployment management, and elements of programme and risk management. It is the key facilitator for meaningful risk-based management decision-making. It provides guidance on managing the complexity related to changes to services and service management processes while preventing undesired consequences and allowing for innovation. This publication also introduces the Knowledge Management process and the Service Knowledge Management System (SKMS), which broadens the use of service and configuration information into knowledge capability for decision and management of services.

At the heart of the ITIL configuration management process is the Configuration Management Database (CMDB). The CMDB may be a single physical repository of configuration information or an integrated set of physical databases and repositories. It is a repository for assets, configuration items (CIs) and the relationships between them. To be effective it requires a system to deliver usable information and processes to maintain the integrity of the configuration items, components, data, information and tools. This publication deals with implementing an effective and useful CMS, including the processes it involves. All changes to service assets and configuration items are recorded in the CMS.

Following from the ITIL vision, this publication also covers the achievement of desirable 'business outcomes' from configuration management, not just the configuration management of IT systems as an end in itself. Nevertheless, it is intended to be useful for any CMS implementation, even one outside the ITIL framework. It is also independent of any vendor-sponsored process and specific configuration management solutions or tools.

The context for this publication is provided by the plenary sessions at the 2008 BCS/itSMF conference, dealing with place of the CMS in business service delivery.

The general objectives of this work is to identify the likely barriers to implementing a CMDB/CMS (in the 21st century) and provide pragmatic 'good practice' approaches to overcoming them using, for example, an ITIL-compliant CMS and SKMS.

Throughout the book, portions of text have been taken directly from ITIL manuals. This text is indicated by the use of quotation marks and the † symbol. All definitions, which are given in the Glossary and appear in boxes in the text, are taken directly from the OGC source material.

# 1 INTRODUCTION

The text of this chapter is formed from a presentation on the Configuration Management System (CMS) that was given by Shirley Lacy and Ivor Macfarlane, co-authors of the ITIL Service Transition publication, at the start of the 2008 itSMF CMSG Conference. It provided the context for the conference as a whole and for the interactive sessions. The latter form the basis for this publication.

## INTRODUCTION TO THE CMS

### The ITIL CMDB

The introduction covered current thinking on why people and organisations think they need a Configuration Management Database (CMDB) solution – that is, a CMS. Typical reasons include support for inventory and asset management, governance and compliance, and simply ITIL best practice implementation. Many organisations want to create a better capability to support service delivery by integrating data and information across multiple sources and providing higher levels of automation for improved performance management.

The rationale for extending the concept of the CMDB in ITIL v3 was covered in the session. In ITIL v2, the definition of a CMDB was: †"…a database that contains all relevant details of each Configuration Item (CI) and details the important relationships between CIs". Although the ITIL v2 configuration management chapter described this as a logical database that could comprise many federated physical CMDBs, people often think that there is just **one** physical CMDB. This view is often encouraged by vendors trying to market their solutions. Believing that the CMDB must always be one physical database often becomes a barrier to implementation because the management buy-in and investment for a single CMDB is too great a challenge for some medium to large organisations.

Another implementation barrier is believing (mistakenly) that auto-discovery tools provide a 'magic' solution. Some marketing and sales people encourage this in order to sell their tools. Although auto-discovery tools can provide an efficient way of obtaining an up-to-date view of the IT environment, they do not collect data about everything that is needed for good configuration management and they can encourage the collection of unnecessary information. A critical success factor is capturing only data that is required for valid business reasons. Many implementations fail because too much unnecessary data is captured or there is a lack of process supporting CMDB maintenance and data capture.

1

## Why ITIL?

The plenary session summarised the reasons behind ITIL. ITIL was updated in June 2007 in recognition of the advances in technology and emerging challenges for IT service providers that include:

- demonstrating value delivery by integrating business and IT services;
- the drive for innovation and change;
- the move to global sourcing;
- changing architectures, including service-oriented and virtualisation architectures;
- convergence of strategy, governance and management practices to meet compliance and control requirements;
- a greater focus on security and risk management;
- managing complex services and systems, with a consequent need for better impact assessment;
- balancing the needs for stability and change.

The structure of the ITIL is based on the ITIL Service Lifecycle, which contains five elements:

- Service Strategy;
- Service Design;
- Service Transition;
- Service Operation;
- Continual Service Improvement.

The ITIL service portfolio represents all the resources presently engaged or being released in various phases of the service lifecycle. It contains a service catalogue, which provides a central and accurate information set for all services running in production. Each service comprises a number of service assets vital to the running of every organisation. The continual feedback at each stage of the lifecycle enables a service provider to optimise its services from a business perspective throughout the service lifecycle.

## Service Asset and Configuration Management

The Service Asset and Configuration Management (SACM) process (often just called the configuration management process) manages the service assets in order to support the other service management processes. Optimising the performance of service assets and configurations improves the overall service performance while mitigating costs and risks caused by poorly managed assets (e.g. service outages, fines, corrective licence fees and failed audits).

The ITIL configuration management process provides a systematic method of breaking down, identifying and managing complex systems and services. It aims to establish the integrity of all identified service assets and configurations within the IT Services environment and includes the following activities:

- **Configuration planning:** understanding and defining the purpose, scope, objectives, policies and procedures as appropriate and required within the context of your organisation.

- **Configuration identification:** identifying the configuration model, the assets and configuration items (CIs) to be managed, their attributes, associated documentation and relationships to other CIs and records. Establishing unique identifiers for CIs, documentation, forms such as Requests for Change and libraries.

- **Configuration control:** the procedures used to control each CI (i.e. to create, build, install, move, add and modify a CI).

- **Configuration status accounting and reporting:** the recording and reporting of current and historical information on a CI throughout its entire lifecycle, using information held within the CMS and its CMDBs.

- **Configuration verification and audit:** checking the CI data held in the CMDB(s) against what is in the real world.

The CMS incorporates a set of applications, tools and databases for collecting, storing, managing, updating, and presenting data about all configuration items and their relationships including a view of an end-to-end service configuration. Some of these application products interface to point solutions such as software version control, release tools and auto-discovery tools. Understanding where a configuration management tool or CMDB fits into the overall architecture, illustrated in Figure 1.1, will help you to select the best solution for your organisation.

**Figure 1.1** The architectural layers of the CMS

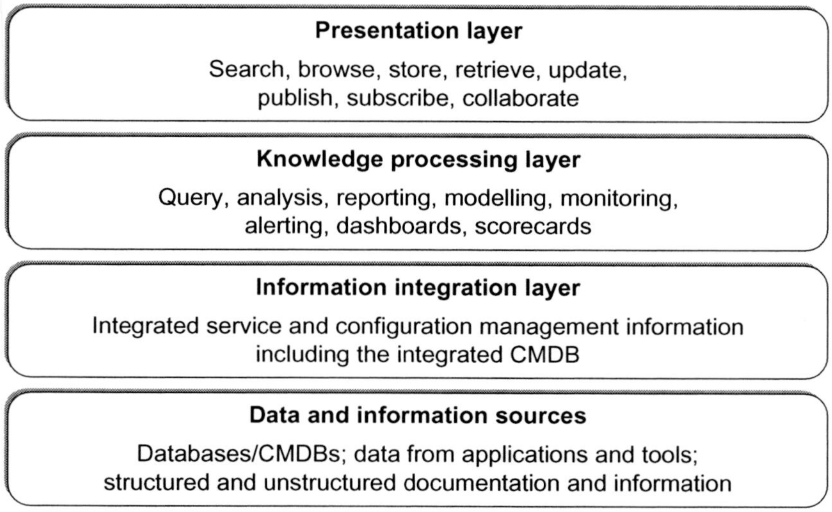

**Presentation layer**

Search, browse, store, retrieve, update,
publish, subscribe, collaborate

**Knowledge processing layer**

Query, analysis, reporting, modelling, monitoring,
alerting, dashboards, scorecards

**Information integration layer**

Integrated service and configuration management information
including the integrated CMDB

**Data and information sources**

Databases/CMDBs; data from applications and tools;
structured and unstructured documentation and information

The processes and functions that comprise configuration management maintain the CMS. The integrated CMDB in the integrated information layer provides the 'single source of truth' about service assets and each configuration item: historical, current and planned. It maps the important relationships between configuration items to deliver a configuration model of an IT service provider's portfolio of services.

The CMS supports all the ITIL process owners, service owners, service management, service operations and IT staff. The CMS is effectively the basis of data and information that supports and facilitates the success and viability of the organisation as a whole, through direct influence and improvement of the ITIL processes. It is the major source of data to allow effective risk management. Without a sound basis for understanding and managing risk, an organisation will be uncompetitive due to an overly conservative risk attitude, or it will be unable to deliver due to excessive risk taking. People need the CMS to perform their IT and service management activities, and also to make informed decisions at appropriate times, for example when assessing the impact of a release going into production or the impact of incidents and problems. People therefore need relevant and accurate configuration data and information in a form that is quick, accessible, easy to update and easy to use and understand, and which is achieved through the presentation layer.

Chapter 2 summarises the feedback from the Conference interactive session about the ITIL practices covered in the plenary.

**KNOWLEDGE CAPTURE DURING THE INTERACTIVE SESSIONS**

The interactive sessions consisted of short 45 minute workshops that harnessed the collective knowledge and experience of the delegates and enabled the capture of a broad body of valuable information for further discussion and analysis.

This interactive approach involved using a combination of collaborative technology (with networked laptops), facilitation and the availability of content experts for each session. The wireless laptops used had specialist software installed to enable ideas, questions and knowledge to be gathered and shared in a fast and efficient manner.

The facilitators led and supported the whole process, providing more in-depth idea generation, deeper group interaction, clearer consensus building and measurement, plus highly efficient documentation of the whole event.

Significant value was added because all participants were able to contribute simultaneously and anonymously. This enhanced the session dynamics of engagement and openness.

The interactive environment demanded a structured and disciplined approach to planning to deliver the best value. During the planning, the outcomes were defined and each session had a customised process depending on the type of session and feedback required. Although the planning was structured, the facilitators were responsive to reshaping and redirecting the sessions as necessary during the conference.

Each session was planned in advance using a combination of methods and techniques selected from the following:

- **Brainstorm:** Delegates brainstormed a specific question and put their responses into category 'buckets'.
- **PMIQ:** Following a presentation or part of a presentation, delegates identified:
  - o PLUS (P) – this is what I liked about what I heard;
  - o MINUS (M) – these are my issues and concerns;
  - o INTERESTING (I) – my insights or points of interest;
  - o QUESTIONS (Q) for the speakers.
- **Stimulus presentation** followed by table discussion and answering specific questions.
- **List:** Delegates were asked to suggest missing items from a list (e.g. a list of users of a CMS).
- **Discussion:** Each table group selected one or two topics from a list to discuss and feedback (e.g. 'What are the barriers to implementing CMS and how can they be overcome?').
- **Gap analysis:** Working in table groups; 'Where are the gaps or weaknesses in XXXX? Explain.'
- **Voting:** Delegates voted individually and the results were displayed immediately as a graph.
- **Question and answer session.**
- **Summary and feedback** on key observations and findings.

The objectives and outcomes for 'implementing a successful CMS' for each day, and the corresponding interactive sessions were:

### Day 1
**Objective:** Successful positioning of CMDB/CMS requires clear explanation of the value to stakeholders. Methods for creating a clear business case were examined and what needs to be overcome in order to implement a CMS successfully was discussed.

**Outcome:** The collective understanding of the value proposition for CMS across a range of organisations and stakeholders was documented. A validated set of key barriers and associated strategies to mitigate these were identified. The document created was made available to participants immediately following the conference.

**What is the CMDB/CMS all for?** A presentation by Shirley Lacy of ConnectSphere and by Ivor Macfarlane of IBM. (Shirley Lacy is a management consultant with a wealth of service and configuration management experience. Ivor Macfarlane is an IT Service Management consultant and trainer working with IBM customers.)

**How can we judge the value of CMDB/CMS?** A presentation by John Dixon of GlaxoSmithKline. (John Dixon was the Director, Quality & Compliance within GlaxoSmithKline's IT Infrastructure Division, involved with managing a project to establish a configuration management function within GSK.)

**CMS: barriers and Critical Success Factors (CSFs)** A presentation by Kevin Holland, NHS Connecting for Health. (Kevin Holland is the Head of Service Quality Improvement for the NHS National Programme for IT.)

**CMS Implementation Case Study** A presentation by Andrew Pieri and Mark Smith of Associated Newspapers Limited (ANL). (Andrew Pieri is Central Operations Director, responsible for Support Service Delivery across ANL's Publishing, Advertising, Commercial and Online business divisions. Mark Smith is Head of Process Management, responsible for the definition, ownership and governance of IS processes.)

**How to improve an existing CM Process** A presentation by John Metcalfe, BCS CMSG and Deirdre Connis, itSMF CCRM Working Party.

**Day 2**
**Objective:** Using shared experiences, how to create alignment between stakeholder requirements and vendor products in CMDB/CMS implementations was debated.

**Outcome:** Structured strategies to close the gap between stakeholder needs and vendor offerings were documented.

**Service Management requirements for the CMDB/CMS** A presentation by Ian Salvage, then of IBM, now of ITAdapt Consultancy Ltd (Ian Salvage was a consultant for IBM's Global Technology Services in the field of Service Management for over 10 years. He has a very broad experience of working across multiple industries delivering IT Service Management solutions to customers.)

**Service Asset and Configuration Management Visions and Strategies** A presentation by Mike Tomkinson, BT Global Services. (Mike Tomkinson is the Configuration Management Beacon for BT Global Services, acting as the touch point for all issues related to CM across the business where required.)

**How do you populate your CMDB?** A presentation by Harvey Davison of Lloyds TSB. (Harvey Davison is the full-time Configuration Manager, designing and implementing a CMDB for LloydsTSB, primarily to support the incident, problem and change processes, one of the foundations for LloydsTSB achieving ISO/IEC 20000 certification.)

**Bringing the CMS to fruition** A presentation by Mark Bools of Principia IT. (Mark Bools has been involved with configuration management for large and small organisations, on projects, programmes and at the corporate strategic level for over 20 years.)

**Selecting CMS tools** A presentation by John Metcalfe of Mentor IT. (John Metcalfe has over 25 years of experience in IT applications. He has provided guidance to IS department management in the development and implementation of strategies for improving change, configuration and release management (CCRM) policies, processes and tool selection to deliver return on investment and benefits to the business.)

**Implementation: what works and what doesn't** A presentation by Shirley Lacy of ConnectSphere and Ian Salvage then of IBM.

A feedback session from the interactive sessions was presented in the main conference room at the end of each day. This was followed by a question and answer session. Most people, regardless of background, level or role, were motivated by this different way of working because they felt engaged with the process. Feedback from delegates at the conference is summarised in Chapter 12.

## ACKNOWLEDGEMENTS

### Session presenters
The CMSG would like to thank the following people for their presentations and general contributions to the 2008 conference:

- Mark Bools, Principia IT;
- Deirdre Connis, itSMF CCRM;
- Harvey Davison, LloydsTSB;
- John Dixon, GlaxoSmithKline;
- Kevin Holland, NHS Connecting for Health;
- Shirley Lacy, ConnectSphere Limited;
- Ivor Macfarlane, IBM;
- John Metcalfe. Mentor IT;
- Andrew Pieri, Associated Newspapers Limited;
- Ian Salvage, then IBM;
- Mark Smith, Associated Newspapers Limited;
- Mike Tomkinson, BT Global Services.

The interactive sessions were designed by:

- Sarah Boulton, Director and Founder of Realise Group Consulting Ltd. Sarah specialises in organisational development consulting, facilitation and coaching. She has over 15 years of experience with companies as diverse as British Airways, BT, BP, BDP Media Group, Rolls Royce, eircom, Inter-American Development Bank and the NHS. Sarah facilitates workshops using RealTools, an innovative group engagement technology that enables sessions to be more open, productive and compelling. She holds postgraduate qualifications in Organisational Behaviour and Psychotherapy.

- Shirley Lacy, of the BCS CMSG and the itSMF. Shirley is Vice Chair of the BCS CMSG. She represents the BCS on the BSI committee that develops the IT service management standard, ISO/IEC 20000. She holds the ITIL Expert accreditation and is an accredited ITIL trainer. She regularly organises and facilitates workshops.

- Nick Leigh, Director of TheReallyUseful.com Ltd. Nick specialises in the design and delivery of workshops and events using interactive technology and collaborative processes. Laptop-based collaborative processes enable large groups to rapidly brainstorm ideas, share information, problem solve, and feedback in an open and transparent way leading to a richer outcome for a meeting. Over 10 years, Nick has designed and delivered hundreds of interactive meetings, workshops and events of all sizes, both face to face and remote.

# 2    THE 21st-CENTURY CMDB/CMS

## OBJECTIVES

This chapter is derived from the first interactive session at the conference.
This followed the plenary session that covered the CMDB/CMS and what
configuration management (CM) has become in the 21st century. The objectives
of this chapter are to review why organisations use a CMS and the initial
barriers to starting a CMS implementation. It also identifies key deliverables
that can be used to stimulate 'buy-in' to the project at all levels.

## SUMMARY

This chapter sets the scene for the rest of the book by presenting the accepted
view of the CMS and what it is for. The interactive sessions then explore any
issues with this.

## THE NORMATIVE VIEW OF WHAT A CMS IS FOR

A presentation by Lacy and Macfarlane: co-authors of the ITIL v3 Service
Transition volume. They led the assembled delegates through the Configuration
Management System (CMS) and the anticipated barriers to its implementation,
as a preliminary to the open discussion on the subject.

The CMS primarily supports asset and configuration management by enabling
an organisation to identify, control, report and audit assets and configurations,
and to manage changes (see Chapter 1). It incorporates a set of applications, tools
and databases for collecting, storing, managing, updating and presenting data
about all configuration items and their relationships, including a view of an
end-to-end service configuration. Some of these application products interface to
point solutions such as software version control, release tools and auto-discovery
tools. The CMS is maintained by the configuration management process and/or
function. The CMS also contributes business benefit via other service management (and wider) processes, facilitating their effectiveness and efficiency. For
example, configuration management delivers the means to achieve impact
analysis for incident and change management, and trend analysis within problem
management. This secondary role has, in the past, to an extent hidden the crucial
role a CMS plays in an organisation.

People use the CMS to perform their IT and service management activities and also to make informed decisions at appropriate times. Key stakeholders for the CMS are therefore the ITIL process owners, service owners, service management, service operations and IT staff.

ITIL presents the CMS architecture in four layers to help people understand the scope and applicability of different CMS applications and tools. They need relevant and accurate configuration data and information in a form that is quick, accessible, easy to update and easy to use and understand. This is achieved through the presentation layer of the CMS shown in Figure 2.1.

The integrated CMDB in the information integrated layer of Figure 2.1 provides the 'single source of truth' about service assets and each configuration item: historical, current and planned. It also maps the important relationships between configuration items to deliver a configuration model of an IT service provider's portfolio of services.

**Figure 2.1** Four architectural layers of the CMS and SKMS

**Presentation layer (Layer 1)**

Search, browse, store, retrieve, update,
publish, subscribe, collaborate

**Knowledge processing layer (Layer 2)**

Query, analysis, reporting, modelling, monitoring,
alerting, dashboards, scorecards

**Information integration layer (Layer 3)**

Integrated service and configuration management information
including the integrated CMDB

**Data and information sources (Layer 4)**

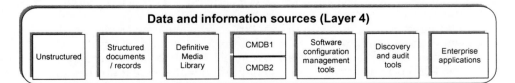

| Unstructured | Structured documents / records | Definitive Media Library | CMDB1 / CMDB2 | Software configuration management tools | Discovery and audit tools | Enterprise applications |

The layers of the CMS and SKMS shown in Figure 2.1 are:

- **Presentation layer (Layer 1):** This layer presents information to users to enable them to do their activities such as searching and finding specific configurations, updating information, reporting, and publishing information and reports. Example users might be operations staff who need to understand the impact of incidents and changes, and software asset management staff who need to audit the software licences.

- **Knowledge processing layer (Layer 2):** This layer collates information to pass to Layer 1. An example might be a tool that analyses information to find the likely sources of unauthorised changes and software licence compliance issues.

- **Information integration layer (Layer 3):** This layer integrates data and information from Layer 4. This layer holds definitive configuration information for the CMS in an integrated CMDB that can be used by Layers 1 and 2. For example the integrated CMDB can integrate application data with infrastructure data to create the configuration information for an end-to-end service.

- **Data and information sources (Layer 4):** These are the definitive sources of data and information that are maintained from different internal and external suppliers. It includes platform specific CMDBs (e.g. on Unix or the mainframe platform) and the Definitive Media Libraries (DMLs) that store definitive master sources of electronic or physical objects such as source code, executable files, software licence documentation and CD-ROMs.

ITIL recognises the broader role of knowledge management within the delivery and support of services. The real value of the CMS is as a fundamental element within a business-focused Service Knowledge Management System (SKMS – illustrated in Figure 2.2). The SKMS stores, manages, updates and presents all information that an IT service provider needs to manage the full lifecycle of IT services. It covers a much wider base of knowledge than the CMS, for example it includes the experience of staff. The decision-making process should be used to drive the design of the SKMS and the CMS.

---

**Figure 2.2** The role of the SKMS and CMS in decision-making

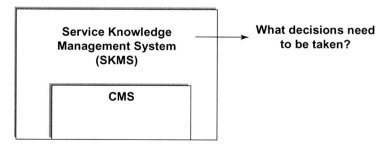

The SKMS lets a vast amount of (relatively) easily collected data to be processed through the information and knowledge layers into delivering the wisdom (targeted and directed information and knowledge) that forms the real basis for effective business decision-making. This focus on delivering accurate business decisions (the key differentiator for most businesses) has also helped expose the myth that configuration management is facilitated by the successful purchase and implementation of technology in the shape of sophisticated software: one the most persistent and traditional myths around configuration management. Although this has been the approach taken by some organisations for many years, the first and most powerful step in the development and implementation of configuration management is the planning (i.e. determining the constraints, what the CMS will cover, what its purposes are, how the information will be maintained etc.).

The tradition of technological focus has led to organisations acquiring and populating CMDB technology without really considering its use or its possible impact on the business. The fact that this CMDB-centric view fits with the marketing strategies of some vendors who have a CMDB to sell has fuelled the fire over recent years. In fact, the CMS and SKMS need to be process-oriented and there are simply no technological 'silver bullets' that will solve the real issues.

Understanding the role that the CMS and broader SKMS can play in an organisation and how the data collected must support and help bond the wide range of required processes are key. Often consultancy, to help change the mindset, rather than improvements in technology, can offer the best chance of something approaching a 'silver bullet'. This is because the successful CMS/SKMS approach requires an 'ITIL culture', or something of similar maturity, which helps organisations focus on business success metrics, on whole lifecycle delivery cost/value, and which considers all the stakeholders in configuration management, not just operations staff. This also helps to avoid collecting data for its own sake.

Establishing the knowledge focus allows an organisation to determine its configuration requirements by reference to its business goals, the business services that support the goals, and the IT and other services that in turn support those business services. Starting at the business end and driving from there, via the service structure, to the data requirements, establishes a CMS approach that:

- collects only data that will be used to support business objectives: not wasting resources on collecting data that will never be used or cannot be maintained;
- ensures that technology purchases reflect what is required and justified;
- allows non-technology data and information to be collected and held within the SKMS and CMS;
- facilitates the use of relevant data and information in support of non-IT services.

## CONTRIBUTORS TO THE INTERACTIVE SESSION

Twenty-three contributing delegates from the practitioner community included representatives from Principia IT, LFEPA, Bloor, Fujitsu Services, Mediatek, BAA, HMPS, Lloyd's of London, BAE Systems, EADS DS UK Ltd, iCore, Teliasonera, Eracent, Shell, Prudential, Stannah, ECB, and Axios Systems.

## PARTICIPATING PRACTITIONER COMMUNITY FEEDBACK

### Barriers to implementation

The delegates were asked to consider and discuss the question 'What are the common problems in implementing a CMDB/CMS?'. Feedback was collected under the headings:

- Demonstrating value/benefit;
- Stakeholders;
- Requirements;
- Design;
- Realisation;
- Other.

### Common problems in implementing a CMDB/CMS

Delegates thought that the benefits of a CMS are often difficult to sell because they are often indirect or intangible. IT people (who often, wrongly, see the CMS in terms of 'their' CMDB) are often poor at communicating the benefits in any case.

It is important to be able to demonstrate the value or benefit of your CMS in business terms, so delegates thought that you should establish useful metrics from the start. You must cover the bigger picture, always remembering that the ultimate (business) client may not have much idea of what a CMS can do for them.

One danger is that the CMS is often implemented to provide compliance with company governance standards or to gain certification against standards, without any real thought as to how the business will benefit. In other words, sometimes people implement a CMS 'because it's the right thing to do', but they don't think about what it could achieve for the business. You must be able to tell the CMS story in language that business stakeholders can understand and you must be able to produce simple cost–benefit examples appropriate to each stakeholder. In the end, everybody involved in implementing a CMS needs to know 'what's in it for me' in order to commit to involvement.

Ultimately, you must be able to persuade people to use the CMS and maintain the CMDB. This means coping with the unfortunate fact that the theory often differs from reality when implementing a real CMS, especially when implementing it in a complex real-world organisation with extensive legacy technologies to replace or integrate with.

## Common stakeholder-related issues in implementing a CMDB/CMS

A common problem delegates found is that senior stakeholders in management can 'talk the talk' without really investing in the process and people issues surrounding the CMS. They sometimes appear to think that buying the right tool (e.g. a new CMDB or auto-discovery tool) is all that is necessary for success.

On the other hand, each organisational silo often wants its own CMDB and process in order to maintain control of its own information. This probably reflects an organisation at a low level of organisational maturity, leading to lack of confidence in other teams outside its own. Previous experience of failures with organisation-wide initiatives is also a barrier for some people.

It is vital to get informed senior management buy-in and to identify the key influencers who can get the business to understand the value of what is proposed and sign off the various commitments needed. You must identify and get the support of the right stakeholders, those who stand to gain by the implementation and also those who hold the key to removing any barriers.

The biggest stakeholder problems you will meet are probably due to a lack of suitable or knowledgeable people in the appropriate areas and to a lack of management and user buy-in. A little knowledge, however, is a dangerous thing, and stakeholders with a small amount of experience or training can hold dangerous misconceptions and sometimes use obfuscating jargon as a defence or barrier to being seen as incompetent or simply unaware of state-of-the-art process.

Ultimately, however, the delegates thought that the key to managing the stakeholder-related issues associated with implementing a CMS is to understand who will pay for the implementation and make sure the resources you will need for it are firmly and formally allocated in the appropriate budgets.

## Common requirement-related problems in implementing a CMDB/CMS

The primary concern here seemed to be with getting the scope of the CMS implementation correct, that is 'What CIs do we need to know about?'. Continual scope creep, both from customers and users, can be an issue, but, according to some delegates, the final scope is usually wider than originally thought. Prioritisation is important: you must capture only what is really required for your CMS, not just whatever is available.

The time frame for implementing a CMDB is often unrealistic and perhaps this is related to unrealistic scoping.

There are sometimes mismatches between the expectations held by the various stakeholders. It's good to have a firm (but negotiable) specification at the start of any phase of a CMS implementation to ensure that all areas are covered to everybody's satisfaction.

## Common design-related problems in implementing a CMDB/CMS

Delegates said that it can be an issue knowing where to start with assets and/or stakeholders. You need to know what, in your organisation, needs to be controlled and where this information is currently held. Legacy silos within the company can create difficult CMDB design issues, redundancy in existing CIs and issues with deleting obsolete CIs. It is also important to get the scope and depth of configuration items correct. If the level is too high the information may not be useful, but too much detail means that you will drown in detail with an expensive maintenance overhead.

Designing the appropriate CI granularity can be difficult: it must be balanced between a technical and a business focus, and kept at a manageable level. The identification of what constitutes a CI will be specific to a given organisation.

The complexity of information and communications technology services can make design difficult and a technical architecture supporting discovery automation, reconciliation and integration with change and other processes (to facilitate maintenance) is not easily available at a reasonable price.

Part of the design phase should be the creation of an appropriate data model, which pulls together the IT design requirements with the requirements from other areas such as Finance, Commercial etc.

## Common problems in implementing a CMDB/CMS associated with realisation

A realisation that 'one size does not fit all' is important. Try starting small and see what can be done without massive investment. This enables faster buy-in from stakeholders.

Tool scalability can be an issue, but do not forget scaling down: delegates pointed out that some tools are not scalable for SMEs. Vendor tool lock-in (e.g. from the service desk area) can also be an issue. Vendors say they have open interfaces, but so far this has not been well demonstrated. And, of course, there is the 'buy it or build it' issue to resolve.

Data quality can be a huge issue: how to ensure it; how to measure it; how to maintain its quality and consistency. Distributed data sources and lack of format commonality can be real issues if you haven't planned for them. A general lack of integration tools for various CMDB sources does not help.

Legacy systems can be a problem too. Most organisations have too many existing systems already embedded into existing processes. You need to maximise the appropriate utilisation of the different legacy 'CMDBs' (or configuration files) while still allaying fears of possible staff redundancy, but gathering all the correct information about certain CI types in disparate environments may not be easy.

In the end, it is important to focus on what you really want from your CMDB/CMS, and make sure that it does it.

### Other common problems in implementing a CMDB/CMS
Choosing the wrong approach can be fatal. Delegates agreed that a gradual (evolutionary) approach is a much lower risk than a big bang (revolutionary) approach.

A lack of adequate resources is often an issue, but the biggest barriers are probably organisation and cultural change. It can be useful to make use of non-IT examples, such as automotive production or using and refining a food recipe, to illustrate the role and benefits of configuration management.

### Specific likes, dislikes and insights arising from the session
Delegates seemed to appreciate reassurance that they are on the correct course and that the industry is generally behind initiatives such as ITIL v3. The need for an additional 'comfort factor' when moving from a technology silo 'comfort zone' to a model encompassing the whole business should not be overestimated. Delegates thought that this CMSG/itSMF event, for example, was pulling unique people with shared interests together, so that they can find out that they are not alone. This probably underlines the importance of giving the people involved in implementing your CMS access to a wider community, whether through face-to-face courses, seminars, BCS events or conferences.

Delegates also appeared to see ITIL v3 as an improvement, commenting that 'it is much more integrated than v2, it looks at the bigger picture and the interfaces between the different areas of service management'. Participants appreciate the ITIL structures and models generally, being able to 'put things in the right place'. ITIL v3 provides a framework that encourages people to think about the end result they expect from configuration management. The outputs include: views and reports, and quality and assurance improvements. Some delegates could already see benefits from implementing CMS in their organisations using the ITIL models.

However, some delegates expressed a concern that the information presented was at a very high level and that, although it all looked good on the diagram, implementation may be too challenging. It appeared rather complex and the models were sometimes incomplete or had too much in them (a difficult balancing act). Some delegates thought that the scope of ITIL v3 is too big and the technology is not yet ready to achieve it.

What are really, in effect, cultural issues were mentioned: the danger of the CMDB becoming an end in itself and the difficulty of measuring improvement when very limited configuration management capabilities are in place to start with. Almost anything, good or bad, can look like an immediate improvement in these circumstances, even if it causes problems in the longer term. Issues may arise when attempting to show management that CMS is the best way forward, when little process or standards are in place (i.e. no ITIL processes are being used).

One possible technology-related barrier was thought to be that many IT people see software configuration management as all there is to configuration management. Another was that a central CMDB may be seen as an unacceptable security risk if you cannot enable secure role-based access to the CMS.

Some very interesting insights came out, especially that the service knowledge concept can usefully be applied at the application level. ITIL v3 can be applied at the application development and business levels.

Some participants wondered about the application to smaller organisations. Some delegates asked whether a specialised CMDB tool is always needed or whether a spreadsheet could do the job, and whether, in a small organisation, a single CMDB product could embody both CMDB and CMS. The answer is yes, in both cases, but you need to fully understand the concepts behind CMS and establish the right process if you are to make a success of this.

### Specific issues identified

Participants were asked to identify specific issues that would need to be addressed during any practical CMS implementation so the feedback could be prioritised and the key issues highlighted, making sure that none were overlooked.

- Delegates thought that the normative model presented is all very well, but people will need to see practical examples of its implementation before trusting it fully.

- There is a possible issue with using the Intellectual Property Rights associated with the published ITIL models (these are explained at www.itil-officialsite.com/nmsruntime/saveasdialog.asp?lID=175&sID=139). Obviously ITIL has worth and if it is given away for no charge, it may not be valued, but the world would benefit if it was more widely adopted. It would be useful if ITIL and other standards, while fully chargeable to organisations, could be made available at discounted prices to individuals.

- There is a small-scale ITIL implementation, but a 'dummies guide' for small organisations would be appreciated to explain CM concepts to non-technical management. These are the sort of things that will appear in the ITIL supplementary materials and ITIL Live. Nevertheless, if an ITIL v3 practitioner cannot explain configuration management to a business manager, perhaps s/he isn't fully trained in ITIL v3 yet!

- Identifying a good starting point for converting those reluctant to change to new ways of working was thought to be a possible issue. As usual, managing change, and especially cultural change, will be the biggest barrier to implementation. In particular, how do you stop the CMDB becoming an end in itself?

- Technical issues identified included the possible administrative burden of a CMS. It is not the cost of implementation that matters in the end but the continuing maintenance cost. A CMS with incomplete information won't be used; but neither will a CMS with so much information that no one can afford to maintain it and it becomes out of date.

- Another technical issue raised is to do with how commercial products map onto ITIL terms such as CMDB, for example the question 'Can IBM ClearCase/Quest be a CMDB?' was asked. To some extent, this needs to be addressed by vendors. There is also the ITIL Software Scheme that vendors can use to certify their software solutions. There are issues with terminology, but hopefully international standards and the ITIL glossary can help with this.

## CONCLUSION

The presenters disposed of the myth that configuration management is simply a matter of the successful purchase and implementation of technology in the shape of sophisticated software.

The CMS is now recognised as a key element of the necessary decision-support system on which the effective delivery of services rests. Although this was always true, the higher profile afforded by the take-up of revised guidance has brought this to the attention of management and this is an important factor in making it more possible to obtain funding to implement an effective CMS. The CMS is central to successful IT service management.

The first and most important step in the development and implementation of configuration management is in identifying the constraints, planning for what the CMS will cover, what it will be used for and by whom.

The interactive discussions covered the key areas of CMS implementation, utilisation and maintenance. They identified issues with demonstrating the value of the CMS to the business (a CMS has no value in itself and is only of value if it is used by the business); with obtaining the right kind of stakeholder buy-in (senior management buy-in is particularly important); designing the appropriate level of granularity for CIs (not so high level as to be useless, but not so low level as to be an unacceptable maintenance overhead); the importance of data quality and of integrating legacy systems; and the importance of dealing with cultural issues.

General issues were identified with the amount of detailed practical assistance available for implementing a CMS and with the difficultly of mapping vendor claims for products onto ITIL requirements.

The issues raised in this chapter will be addressed in later chapters.

# 3   JUDGING THE VALUE OF CMDB/CMS

**OBJECTIVES**

The objectives of this chapter are to identify and prioritise the value of a CMDB/CMS for its key stakeholders.

**SUMMARY**

This chapter documents the value that practitioners expect from their CMS (based both on an ongoing external survey and facilitated delegate discussion) and shows that the anticipated benefits are largely in line with those predicted by ITIL and are measurable. Nevertheless, they are of a kind where it can be hard to calculate a formal return on investment.

A rich list of possible stakeholders who might see this value was documented and the organisational structures in which CMS relates to these stakeholders was reported. The value to the senior management team was explored in some depth.

**THE VALUE OF A CMS**

From his practical experience as one-time Director, Quality & Compliance, IT Systems and Communication Services at GlaxoSmithKline, John Dixon was particularly well placed to highlight the value, or otherwise, of the CMS. Value is always harder to measure than costs, but if you want to improve your processes, increasing value is often more productive as a driver than cutting costs (partly because cutting costs too far can impact the value delivered quite badly).

In 1998, GlaxoWellcome (as it was then) had no central, robust inventory of its IT assets and its change management process was based on a 'paper and spreadsheet' approach. A small group of GlaxoWellcome employees decided that something better and more automated was needed and gained somewhat grudging support from senior management for them to 'build something'. Clearly, a strong 'value' story at this point might have got more commitment from senior managers.

An in-house tool called Chameleon (which registered configuration items, documented the relationships between them and managed the workflow for changes) was built as a 'proof of concept' while the business case for a commercial tool was prepared.

Chameleon was expected to last two years. It is now over 10 years later and after the merger of GlaxoWellcome with SmithKline Beecham to form GSK in 2000, Chameleon is still in use for over 100,000 employees, over 7,500 servers, over 250 networks and some 80,000 desktops.

This probably means that it is delivering value. The CMSG finds that, in general, people who have an effective CMS in their organisation would be loath to give it up. However, no matter how attractive a CMS seems to be, when it actually comes down to implementing a solution (together with its associated tools, organisations and structures) someone is going to have to sign a fairly large cheque. At this point, you need to be able to justify the spend more formally (in terms of return on investment and/or improvements to key processes) than by simply saying that the CMS is a 'no brainer'.

While doing a master's degree, John Dixon started to research some key aspects of justifying the value of GSK's investment in its CMS. John could not get all the data he needed out of the current system and the data he could get was not accurate (72 per cent at best). The only cost–benefit analyses available came from vendors (with their own agendas) and tended to concentrate on greenfield sites. John was driven by frustration at his inability to do his Quality & Compliance job properly within these constraints.

Catalysed by the requirements of his MSc work as well, John decided to research some key questions:

- Does configuration management add value and how has it been implemented across IT service organisations?
- What, if any, are the business benefits in implementing configuration management and can they be articulated?
- What sort of organisational model is being used to support configuration management?

John wants his research to benefit GSK, which faces a daunting challenge: the management of such a large and complex estate, especially when regulatory compliance is added to the mix. His work is largely based on a survey (readers can contribute to the survey itself at www.surveymonkey.com.

The questionnaire consists of a combination of five-point Likert-scale questions (see www.socialresearchmethods.net/kb/scallik.php), voting (closed) questions, some open-ended questions, and options to add clarifying data. The questionnaire is split into four sections, with the first two sections being used to understand the scale and complexity of the organisations participating in the survey, which could then be used to compare GSK against the sample.

- The first section collects basic demographic information:

  - Name;
  - Address;
  - Size;
  - Geographic coverage;
  - Regulatory implications.

- The second section covers information about the IT department:

  - Type of department;
  - Size;
  - Number of users;
  - Number of staff;
  - Complexity of the infrastructure;
  - Number of data centres;
  - Amount of outsource support.

- The third section covers how configuration is addressed within the organisation:

  - Approach to configuration management;
  - Technology support of configuration management;
  - Historical development of configuration management;
  - Acquisition of tools and standards/certification within the organisation.

- The fourth section looks at the benefits seen through implementing configuration management:

  - Drivers for implementation;
  - Formality of initiation of configuration management;
  - Results of expected benefits;
  - Value gained from configuration management and unexpected benefits.

Dixon's study focuses on a relatively small group of IT service industry organisations and his research indicates that in the configuration management community as a whole (with some caveats):

- Only 14 per cent have a fully defined business case with articulated return on investment (ROI) and Key Improvement Indicators or metrics.

- 45 per cent do not have a formal project to implement configuration management, instead it has grown organically.

- An overwhelming 90.4 per cent stated they had acquired tools to support configuration management implementation.

However, half of the survey respondents say that they do not have tools to verify/validate their CMDB data, which, it seems to us, ought to be one of the key benefits from a CMS solution.

Dixon started his conference session by asking the assembled delegates to vote on the question 'Where are you today in implementing configuration management?'.

- 21.4 per cent said that they had started from a greenfield situation ('It was a difficult project starting from nothing or very little'), and roughly the same number (19 per cent) said, 'It was a project based on an already existing process and/or tools.'
- 45 per cent claimed that configuration management had just 'grown, like Topsy' ('It has developed over time with business need but without a formal project.') This is worrying because, although configuration management is presumably meeting a need, it is presumably also at risk from cost cutting etc. It would seem to be a good idea to document a formal business case based on value delivered, in advance of someone unsympathetic not finding one!

Dixon's research is an ongoing project, but so far it seemed that the CMSG delegates were fairly typical of the configuration management community in general.

### ITIL value statements

Part of Dixon's survey explores whether the ITIL descriptions of the value of the CMS are valid in the industry. At this stage, it is worth mentioning that ITIL documents the expected value to the business in the Service Transition volume for change and configuration management, Sections 4.2.3 and 4.3.3, as shown in Tables 3.1 and 3.2.

---

**Table 3.1** ITIL value statements for configuration management (Source: OGC Service Transition ISBN 978-0-113310-48-7)

---

1    Better forecasting and planning of changes.

2    Changes and releases to be assessed, planned and delivered successfully.

3    Incidents and problems to be resolved within the service level targets.

4    Service levels and warranties to be delivered.

5    Better adherence to standards, legal and regulatory obligations (less non-conformances).

6    More business opportunities as able to demonstrate control of assets and services.

7    Changes to be traceable from requirements.

8    The ability to identify the costs for a service.

---

**Table 3.2** ITIL value statements for change management (Source: OGC Service Transition ISBN 978-0-113310-48-7)

| 1 | Prioritising and responding to business and customer change proposals. |
|---|---|
| 2 | Implementing changes that meet the customers' agreed service requirements while optimising costs. |
| 3 | Contributing to meet governance, legal, contractual and regulatory requirements. |
| 4 | Reducing failed changes and therefore service disruption, defects and re-work. |
| 5 | Delivering change promptly to meet business timescales. |
| 6 | Tracking changes through the Service Lifecycle and to the assets of its customers. |
| 7 | Contributing to better estimations of the quality, time and cost of change. |
| 8 | Assessing the risks associated with the transition of services (introduction or disposal). |
| 9 | Aiding productivity of staff through minimising disruptions due to high levels of unplanned or 'emergency' change and hence maximising service availability. |
| 10 | Reducing the Mean Time to Restore Service (MTRS), via quicker and more successful implementations of corrective changes. |
| 11 | Liaising with the business change process to identify opportunities for business improvement. |

**Improvements from the CMS**

For the purposes of the questionnaire, Dixon splits out the benefits for items 2 and 5 in the ITIL list of configuration management values (Table 3.1) to provide a greater degree of granularity. Dixon uses the list shown in Table 3.3 for the 11 answer options to the question 'Thinking about the value or benefit gained from your implementation of configuration management, since implementing a configuration management system my organisation has seen improvement in'.

The benefits are shown in ranked order in Figure 3.1. This shows that all 11 change management value statements are endorsed.

In relation to adherence/compliance with regulatory requirements:

- 56.7 per cent of Dixon's respondents cite compliance with regulatory obligations as a benefit (ITIL change management value statement 3);
- avoiding audit non-conformance is also cited (45.9 per cent).

**Table 3.3** Survey value statements for configuration management

| | |
|---|---|
| A | Number of business opportunities through better control of assets and services. |
| B | Adherence/compliance with standards, legal and regulatory obligations. |
| C | Number of audit non-conformances received. |
| D | Forecasting and planning of changes. |
| E | Success of changes. |
| F | Success of releases. |
| G | Traceability of changes from defined requirements. |
| H | Achievement of service levels. |
| I | Number of contractual warranty claims. |
| J | Identifying the cost of its service(s). |
| K | Time taken to resolve incidents. |

Many of the highly ranked value statements cover the benefits related to change and release management that are aligned with the ITIL value statements in configuration management. Section 4.3.3 (shown in Table 3.1) and the ITIL Change Management Section 4.2.3 (shown in Table 3.2):

- 55.5 per cent cite more successful changes (ITIL change management value statements 1, 4 and 5). A low change success rate is one of ITIL's top five risk indicators of poor change management.
- 52.8 per cent also cite achieving service levels (ITIL change management value statements 5 and 9).
- 51.3 per cent also cite change traceability (ITIL change management value statement 6).
- 50 per cent cite change forecasting/planning (ITIL change management value statement 7).

Behind these statements come:

- Release success (47.3 per cent). (ITIL change management value statements 2 and 8).
- Incident resolution time (47.2 per cent). (ITIL change management value statement 10).

The lowest three rankings covered business opportunities, identifying costs and warranty claims:

- Increasing business opportunities through better control (44.5 per cent) (ITIL change management value statement 11).

- Identifying service cost (33.4 per cent) (ITIL change management value statement 7).

- Reducing contractual warranty claims (30.6 per cent), not explicitly mentioned in ITIL but included in some of the values cited by the survey respondents.

It is unsurprising, however, that warranty claims score the lowest in the ranking, because this benefit generally only applies to those organisations providing third-party IT services and the majority of the respondents were internal IT organisations.

**Figure 3.1** Observed benefits of configuration management in ranked order

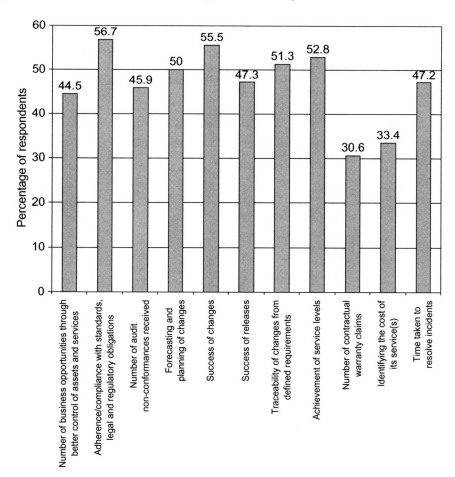

## Organising for configuration management

Figure 3.2 shows that 24.4 per cent of respondents have no people dedicated to configuration management, 29.3 per cent have one or two people, 19.5 per cent have 3–5 people, 19.5 per cent have 6–10 people, and about 7 per cent have 21 or more. The fact that a quarter of respondents do not have a dedicated configuration management team is perhaps a matter for concern because this is hardly a part-time role (except, perhaps, from necessity in the very smallest organisations, which probably have less demanding CMS needs anyway).

Figure 3.3 shows that 58.5 per cent of respondents have a central configuration management department, possibly also with supporting configuration management functions in multiple departments (almost half of these), but rather worryingly, 39 per cent of respondents have no central function and a few (2.4 per cent) claim to have no configuration management function at all.

Figure 3.4 shows that the configuration management role tends not to report at the highest (CEO) level: it mostly reports to a senior manager/director (34.1 per cent) or at a manager level just below this (36.6 per cent). However, perhaps the 7.3 per cent of organisations where CM reports at senior management team level (board director, CIO, SVP, VP) may have its status right. If the configuration management role reports at too low a level, conflicts of interest are likely to make it difficult to manage and its potential value delivery may not be achieved.

---

**Figure 3.2** Number of people (full-time equivalents) dedicated to the configuration management function

| | Response percentage |
|---|---|
| None | 24.4% |
| 1–2 | 29.3% |
| 3–5 | 19.5% |
| 6–10 | 19.5% |
| 11–20 | 0.0% |
| 21 or over | 7.3% |

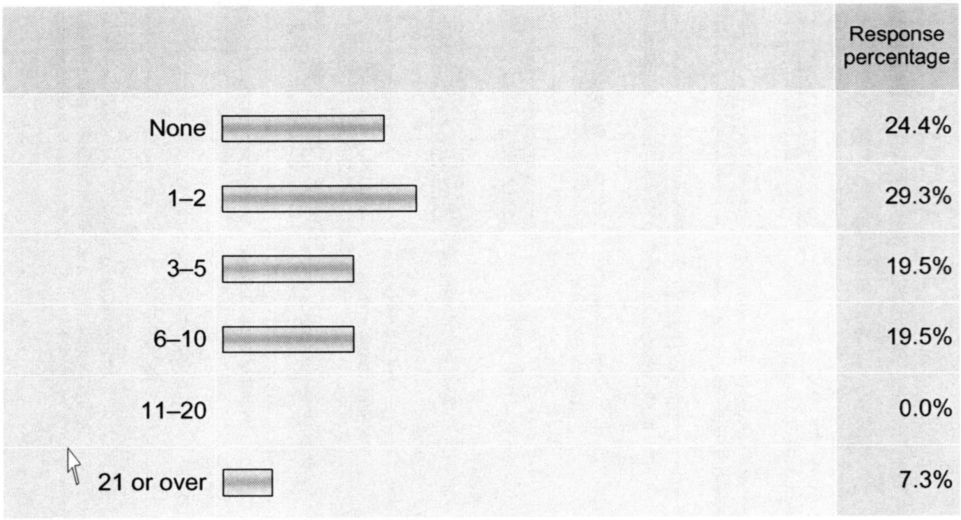

**Figure 3.3** Organisations that have established a function/department for configuration management

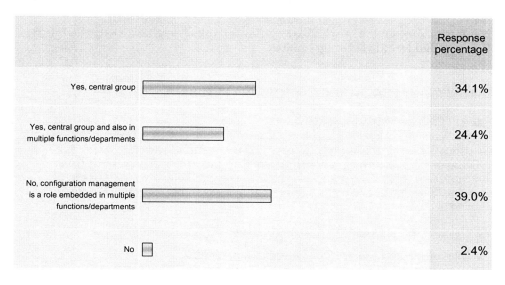

| | Response percentage |
|---|---|
| Yes, central group | 34.1% |
| Yes, central group and also in multiple functions/departments | 24.4% |
| No, configuration management is a role embedded in multiple functions/departments | 39.0% |
| No | 2.4% |

**Figure 3.4** Reporting level for the configuration management role in an IT service organisation

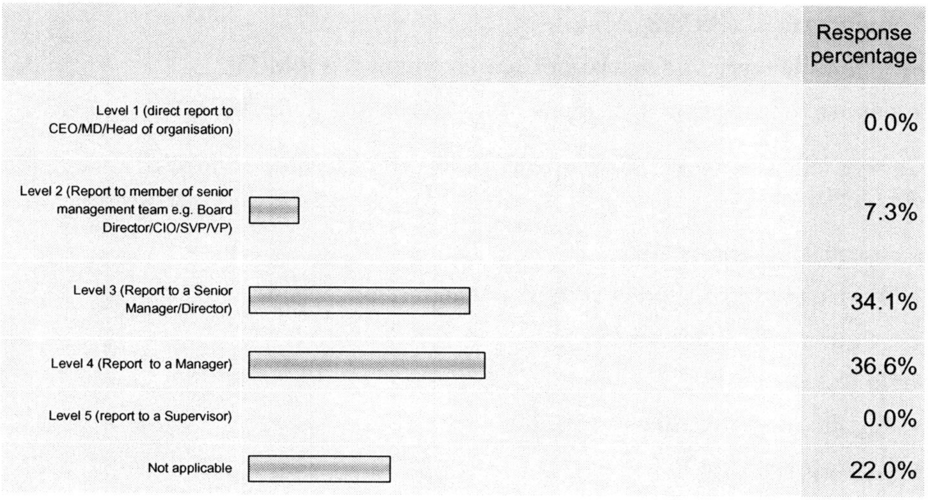

| | Response percentage |
|---|---|
| Level 1 (direct report to CEO/MD/Head of organisation) | 0.0% |
| Level 2 (Report to member of senior management team e.g. Board Director/CIO/SVP/VP) | 7.3% |
| Level 3 (Report to a Senior Manager/Director) | 34.1% |
| Level 4 (Report to a Manager) | 36.6% |
| Level 5 (report to a Supervisor) | 0.0% |
| Not applicable | 22.0% |

## CONTRIBUTORS TO THE INTERACTIVE SESSION

Twenty-one contributing delegates from the practitioner community included representatives from CA, Bloor, EDS, ESA, O2, ECB, Eracent, University of Oxford, NHS Connecting for Health, Unilever, Transport For London, Motability Operations, Atos Origin, ASG, Tideway, Royal Bank of Scotland, Deutsche Bank, Simmons and DeltaRail Group Limited.

## PARTICIPATING PRACTITIONER COMMUNITY FEEDBACK

### Value of CMS for different stakeholders

A prime consideration for identifying the value provided by a CMS is the identification of all the stakeholders who might benefit from this value. If a stakeholder is overlooked, any value that they might be getting is lost from consideration. After hearing about Dixon's research delegates were asked to consider the following list of possible stakeholders in the light of his survey results:

- Organisational compliance/risk management (CCO/CRO);
- Organisational senior management team (SMT);
- Chief Financial Officer (CFO);
- Chief Information Officer (CIO);
- Knowledge management champions (CKO);
- Service improvement/quality improvement management (QM);
- Business relationship management/account management/service level management (BRM/SLM);
- Service delivery and operations management (OPS MGT);
- Service delivery and operations teams/personnel (OPS TEAM);

However, following from the group discussion, the following additional stakeholders were identified:

- Business representatives;
- Service managers and/or process owners;
- Suppliers of services or tools;
- Project managers;
- Regulators (external or internal);
- Tools support staff;
- Service desk personnel or managers;
- Architects (business, solution and technical).

The delegates were then divided into groups and invited to discuss, 'What is the value of CMDB/CMS to your chosen stakeholder group?'. Obviously, not all stakeholders could be considered. Consideration of those not covered here is left 'as an exercise for the reader'.

### The value of CMS for business representatives

Delegates thought that the value of the CMS for business representatives is associated with being able to assess the impact of change and from ensuring that IT remains 'fit for purpose' as business and IT requirements change and evolve.

The CMS also enables the business to be more successful through the effective deployment of IT, assuring:

- improved stability;
- availability;
- agility;
- transparency: openness, cost, performance, risk, values etc.

### The value of CMS for the senior management team

With an effective CMS, delegates thought that the value of the CMS comes from the SMT (Senior Management Team: Board Director, CIO, SVP, VP) being able to see and understand what they are governing as well as the relationship between business processes and the complete IT estate.

The SMT will have more confidence that IT can deliver what is required, because the CMS demonstrates that IT knows what it has, where it is and how it is configured. This leads to fewer failed changes, better confidence in what needs to be purchased, enables leverage of existing assets etc. It also helps to inform the cost attribution processes. The CMS also helps to provide an audit trail for the SMT that specifically supports its regulatory compliance obligations, including those for the maintenance of security and business continuity.

It is particularly important that the value of the CMS for the SMT is expressed in business terms. Thus, the CMS helps to promote business capability/agility (the ability of the business to create new market opportunities) and it increases the availability of services the business depends on, improves the achievement of business-oriented SLAs, reduces support cost overheads and leads to less waste from 'rework' associated with failed change implementations.

A better understanding of the relationship between business processes and the IT estate should also increase the responsiveness of IT Support, because it should be able to prioritise its allocation of resources more in line with the needs of the business. In general allocation of costs to changes, outages and incidents will be more effective.

There is, delegates thought, value for the SMT in being able to treat IT as a 'black box' supplier of business-enabling services. The CMS reduces the risks associated with this through improved change and incident impact assessment. Knowledge of the associations and relationships inherently documented in an effective CMS will allow optimisation of the IT estate for cost control and increased ROI.

The SMT was an important focus for delegates: a focus with which we agree, because effective, informed, committed executive level sponsorship is vital for the effective implementation of the CMS.

### The value of CMS for architects

Delegates thought that the role of architects is, in part, to ensure that the strategic objectives of configuration management align with the strategic objectives of the information management strategy. An effective CMS, that is one in which CIs are within scope and toolsets integrate well, will ensure that the data within the scope of configuration management are of a suitable quality and integrity to support effective strategic decision-making.

### The value of CMS for the change management process owner

According to delegates, an effective CMS should ensure that all changes are traceable and have relationships to the respective incident, problem and release records. The value of this to the change management process owner is that the CMS makes available the appropriate level of information to the right people for them to assess effectively the impact of a particular change based on the risk profile associated with the change.

### The value of CMS for the service desk

Delegates thought that the value of the CMS and its associated CMDB and configuration management to the service desk is that (as a function of incident management) it provides the right (i.e. accurate and up-to-date) information that is needed to ensure that normal service is restored as soon as possible after incident.

### The value of CMS for the project manager

Delegates saw the CMS as an important aspect of fact-based decision-making for project managers. The CMS improves the quality and availability of relevant information throughout the complete service and project lifecycle, thus supporting the delivery of projects on time, to budget and with improved quality.


## CONCLUSION

Dixon's research project explores whether configuration management adds value and whether the benefits of implementing configuration management can be articulated. It also explores how configuration management is implemented across real IT service organisations because this affects the business case for implementation.

Dixon's research and the interactive session confirm that people can articulate the benefits that they expect from configuration management and their CMS. These benefits are largely in line with ITIL 'value to business' statements in the Service Transition volume in the chapters on Change Management and Configuration Management. The observer benefits in decreasing order of importance were:

- adherence/compliance with standards, legal and regulatory obligations;
- success of changes;
- achievement of service levels;
- traceability of changes from defined requirements;
- forecasting and planning of changes;
- success of releases;
- time taken to resolve incidents;
- number of audit non-conformances received;
- number of business opportunities through better control of assets and services;
- identifying the cost of its service(s);
- number of contractual warranty claims.

The first benefit, compliance with standards, legal and regulatory obligations, means that organisations need to establish a basic capability to manage and control IT assets and configurations. This is often a significant challenge, but we have seen many IT organisations do this over the last 10 years as they realise the need for formal governance, risk and compliance initiatives. The benefit would be a reduced number of audit non-conformances received but, clearly, to achieve this benefit it is necessary for compliance audits to be undertaken in the first place.

Many of the benefits from configuration management are realised through other processes such as change management, incident management and service level management. Calculating a formal return on investment, and thus demonstrating hard benefits, can be hard unless there is an integrated approach to implementing these processes with configuration management as a foundation. However, many of these other processes also provide the capability for an organisation to measure the benefits of configuration management.

The findings in Dixon's research and from the interactive session are supported by our industry experience. Organisations implementing ITIL often achieve 20–50 per cent efficiency savings by implementing a set of processes. Often organisations begin with incident, problem and change management and a basic understanding of their services and key assets. These processes help organisations begin to measure the time taken to resolve incidents, the success of changes and releases, and these measures can be used to demonstrate benefits.

In addition, some organisations progress to adding request fulfilment, elements of service level management and a basic service catalogue, to their initial investment in a CMS. This gives them the ability to measure some other benefits, such as achievement of service levels.

Some organisations implement incident, problem and change management with configuration management. The resulting benefits to these organisations is increased change and release success rate, traceability of changes from defined requirements and better forecasting of planning of changes.

Organisations that implement the full set of ISO/IEC 20000 processes have demonstrated significant improvements, and these organisations will also have, in practice, a culture of continual improvement.

The most popular organisational model for the institutionalisation of configuration management is currently one with between 1–10 people split over multiple areas, with configuration managers reporting to a manager. We think that the CMS will be more successful at delivering its potential value if the configuration management role reports to a higher level than this, that is to a member of the senior management team (e.g. the CIO). Senior management encouragement and informed support are important to achieving the potential business value of the CMDB/CMS in practice.

# 4 OVERCOMING THE BARRIERS TO THE CMS

**OBJECTIVES**

This chapter aims to help readers to identify and prioritise Critical Success Factors (CSFs) for the Configuration Management System and to identify barriers to implementing it.

**SUMMARY**

This chapter looks at CSFs and barriers to implementation for the CMS, both generally and for a selection of specific stakeholders in the CMS. It relates the CSFs found in interactive discussion to the CSFs for Service Transition in the ITIL v3 volumes and highlights ITIL v3 CSFs that do not seem to feature strongly in delegates' discussions.

**BARRIERS AND CRITICAL SUCCESS FACTORS**

This section is based on an original presentation by Kevin Holland (of NHS Connecting for Health) who has a reputation for thought leadership in many aspects of the practical application of IT service management theory, and is a well-respected presenter and facilitator.

Holland led a stimulus session and asked the assembled CMSG/itSMF conference delegates whether the CMS was in fact a mythical beast, and, in similar vein, whether the usually accepted barriers to its implementation were fact or fiction.

The problem he highlighted for people implementing a CMS is that perception matters. 'What everyone knows' may not be true and one barrier to CMS success may be that the CMS concept carries some baggage from when configuration management was implemented entirely for the IT group, without much concern for (or recognition of) any business stakeholders. Things are changing, and ITIL v3 is a symptom of this change: from 'aligning IT with the business' (which implies an IT focus) to 'integrating IT with the business' (implying a business focus). However, news of this change of focus may be slow in getting through to some organisations, and promotion of dysfunctional visions may be the result. A CSF is something that must happen if an organisation is to succeed in implementing a plan and, thus, achieve its vision. If the CSFs are not appropriate there is a risk that the implementation may lead to a dysfunctional operational process.

The choice of CSFs depends on the strategic vision behind a CMS initiative. If the CMS (or, more likely, its technology) becomes an end in itself, rather than a business-oriented process improvement project, a chosen CSF might be that the business users are not involved or consulted because they may delay the implementation. However, if the vision is of an institutionalised CMS used by all of its stakeholders, then the opposite is true and the CSFs chosen might be the full involvement of the business and the effective management of change for all stakeholders.

Of course, the IT Group is a stakeholder in the CMS, but only one of many. The obvious question for people wanting to implement an effective CMS is 'Does our CMS strategy deliver any value to the business?'.

However, answering this question in a manner that lets you decide whether your CMS implementation is a success or failure may not be straightforward. For instance, are you dogmatic about what your CMS must do, and if it does not do these things will you decide that it is not a success? Or, alternatively, are you pragmatic: if your CMS does something useful, even if you did not quite anticipate it achieving this, is that fine by you? Or are you somewhere in between? In any case, when will your CMS have enough real, useful information in it to support a useful proportion of your stakeholders? If you set a CSF or Key Performance Indicator (KPI) based merely on the quantity of raw data in a CMDB, it is unlikely that you will be able to demonstrate a real value added to the business by the CMS.

If you are interested in more technical success indicators, does the level at which your assets or configuration items are defined support the delivery of business value, for example? Configuration items should not be so high level that business practitioners cannot relate to them, nor so low level that maintaining them is a major overhead.

Here are two fundamental questions for people seeking to implement a functional CMS: do you understand the needs of your stakeholders; and do you believe in the tool vendors' magic bullets? Perhaps the key CSF for a successful CMS implementation is that you can answer 'yes' to the first and 'no' to the second, before you start.

Consideration of such issues provided the context for the delegates in the interactive session in which to identify useful CSFs for the implementation of a CMS. In addition, the ITIL Service Transition volume documents a set of CSFs for Service Transition (which includes the CMS) in Chapter 9 (section 9.2). These are related to those identified by the delegates below.

## CONTRIBUTORS TO THE INTERACTIVE SESSION

Twenty contributors to the discussion represented the practitioner community. They included representatives from Financial Times, Fidelity Investments,

Cheshire County Council, Tideway, Principia IT, BAE, Mouchel, TfL, Ericsson AB, Monetical Ltd., EADS DS UK Ltd., iCore Ltd., Cheshire Police, Bloor, Motability Operations, Plymouth City Council, GSK, KPMG and Deutsche Bank.

## PARTICIPATING PRACTITIONER COMMUNITY FEEDBACK

### Barriers and Critical Success Factors

At the start of this interactive session, the delegates were asked to pick up to three stakeholders (from the stakeholder list in Chapter 3), choosing those that would benefit the most from the CMS. Delegates were asked to discuss the key CSFs (things that must be present in the organisation before the CMS can be successful) for their particular stakeholders and to explain the reasons for choosing them, explaining the barriers to implementation for that stakeholder group.

Each person voted individually using the interactive technology and the results were displayed immediately on a main screen for Holland and the group to comment on.

### Service and operations teams

The CSFs appropriate for this group were identified as:

- customer/stakeholder satisfaction, leading to continued investment and support for IT and business automation generally;
- a demonstrable ability to predict potential problems more accurately, thus reducing rework and cost;
- a demonstrable ability to optimise service assets and therefore reduce cost to the organisation;
- a demonstrable ability to respond to changing environment quickly and take advantage of business opportunities;
- the meeting or exceeding the provisions of Operational Level Agreements/ Service Level Agreements (OLAs/SLAs) and documented Key Performance Indicators (KPIs), in order to meet contractual/agreed obligations and reduce rework and cost.

These are similar to the following CSFs in ITIL:

- †"Understanding and managing the different stakeholder perspectives that underpin effective risk management within an organisation and establishing and maintaining stakeholder buy-in and commitment.
- Being able to communicate the organisation's attitude to risk and approach to risk management more effectively during Service Transition activities.
- Building a thorough understanding of risks that have impacted or may impact the successful Service Transition of services in the Service Portfolio.
- Developing good quality systems, tools, processes and procedures required to manage a Service Transition practice.

- Demonstrating that the benefits of establishing and improving the Service Transition practice and processes outweigh the costs (across the organisation and services).

- Automating processes to eliminate errors and reduce the cycle time."

Possible barriers to CMS implementation for this group were identified as:

- Time, if the Service and Operations teams are too busy fire fighting. This implies that the maturity needed for operating a CMS, and its corresponding rework-avoidance culture, is missing. Involvement of these teams in the development of the CMS will help, but, fundamentally, there are cultural and senior management buy-in issues to address here.

- A silo mentality, if the CMS is not owned or developed in conjunction with the Service and Operations teams, then people in these teams are unlikely to be interested. This is a fundamental cultural issue but a focus on the distributed ownership of data, accountability and authority may help.

- A lack of trust in the data in the CMS. An explicit (planned and budgeted) focus on maintaining the timeliness and accuracy of this data is needed.

- Cultural barriers. These can be addressed with communication, training and education, and the consideration of ease of use for the target users when acquiring systems for the CMS.

- The CMS is perceived to be bureaucratic and to not add value. This is really another cultural issue and can be addressed with mentoring and training, which shows how the CMS and its associated automation will make the jobs of the Service Operations people easier.

### Service desk
The delegates working on this stakeholder group came out with very specific CSFs that relate to users of the CMS doing their job better. This perhaps reflects the fact that practitioners will understand the benefits if these are articulated in a way that they can relate to their job as opposed to the overall objective.

The CSFs identified here are important, but they are probably more detailed than would be really helpful in selling the CMS to the management team. In fact, they are more a specification for functionality to support a capability, or performance metrics that could be used to demonstrate the overall value of a CMS.

The following CSFs relate to improving performance, effectiveness and efficiency improvements:

- Speed of access to the CMS and near real-time update of its information content.

- Usability/intuitiveness of interface.

- It should be possible to automate frequent tasks.

- Set metrics on the outcomes of implementing changes and resolving incidents.

- Accuracy of information held: the availability of complete, accurate and up-to-date information.

- The CMS should be reliable and the service desk staff should be able to rely on it.
- Quality assurance processes for the CMS should be in place and monitored.
- The CMS should identify trends to feed back to CSI (Continual Service Improvement).

The following CSFs relate to establishing a basic capability or functionality within the CMS:

- Identification of changes that could have resulted in incidents.
- The ability to easily update CI information at the appropriate level.
- Access to solutions identified in similar incidents.
- The ability to keep track of release patches sent out to users' machines.
- The ability to quickly assign an incident to a team.
- The CMS should link to known errors and workarounds.
- Root cause analysis of seemingly unrelated incidents.
- A change history should be maintained.
- The CMS should identify dependencies between CIs to help identify the impact of changes and incidents.
- Removal of the need to go out to users to investigate incidents.

The last of these 'CSFs' is interesting. If a resolving agency can use the information in the CMS to resolve incidents remotely, then the frequency of visits to users can be reduced. This often delivers significant cost savings, sometimes 20–40 per cent of the cost of incident and problem resolution. This can provide immediate justification for a CMS initiative.

The barriers to the service desk accepting the CMS were listed at a similarly detailed level from a user's perspective (or as cultural CSFs):

- Poor tools that are difficult to understand and that do not provide process or support flow diagrams.
- A lack of management buy-in or support and a corresponding lack of any formal process.
- A lack of trust in the CMS because of the poor accuracy of the information in it, or the lack of appropriate information, or the lack of an appropriate level of information.
- Not giving appropriate access to the people who need it.
- Inappropriate and bureaucratic controls, which might place the welfare of the CMS above the welfare of the production service it is supposed to protect (although the implementation of effective controls can be a selling point for the CMS and persuade groups to put their information into it).

- Wrongly focused metrics (such as measuring time to call-out rather than the time to fix the problem so that it stays fixed).
- Training or 'marketing' issues, such as:

  o people not understanding the value of accurate CMS information;

  o people not understanding or sticking to a common usage policy (for categorisation etc.);

  o people simply not understanding the CMS process (feelings that CMS has no practical use, 'it's only data collection'). The importance of a lack of training as a barrier to CMS implementation was emphasised.

- Cultural maturity issues, such as: 'knowledge is power, why share it?', or a desire for the 'comfort' achieved by not abandoning existing processes or repositories.
- Additionally, as usual, the time taken to maintain the CMS, if onerous, is a barrier to adoption.

The related ITIL CSFs are:

- †"Developing good-quality systems, tools, processes and procedures required to manage a Service Transition practice.
- Automating processes to eliminate errors and reduce the cycle time.
- Creating and maintaining new and updated knowledge in a form that people can find and use.
- Understanding and managing the different stakeholder perspectives that underpin effective risk management within an organisation and establishing and maintaining stakeholder buy-in and commitment.
- Developing a workforce with the right knowledge and skills, appropriate training and the right service culture."

No specific barriers to implementation, beyond the issues already mentioned, were identified for this group.

### Service managers/Process owners
The CSFs appropriate to this group were identified as being that the CMS provides:

- assured quality data, because service managers will want to use it to confirm that their process is working correctly;
- timely information (not just timely data) for the incident manager, because the manager needs to be assured that the incident team can act quickly and accurately to resolve all incidents.

The related ITIL CSFs are:

- †"Creating and maintaining new and updated knowledge in a form that people can find and use.

- Developing good-quality systems, tools, processes and procedures required to manage a Service Transition practice.

- Automating processes to eliminate errors and reduce the cycle time."

The barriers to CMS implementation for this group were thought to be:

- flawed processes: the CMS should help to address these by providing a feedback mechanism to help process improvement;

- a lack of senior management buy-in: the CMS should help to address this by allowing multiple views of the same data/information appropriate to different audiences, including senior managers;

- unrealistic expectations of what the CMS can provide and of the amount of commitment needed to maintain it: adopt a pragmatic approach and implement the solution in phases that are realistic and achievable;

- a lack of integrity for the information held in the CMS and insufficient availability of CMS information: focus on the process and people as well as the technology solutions;

- a fear of being held accountable for failure, because of the increased transparency introduced with the CMS: counteract this by building a team and organisation capability with demonstrable improvements in metrics that indicate overall success.

### Service delivery and operations management
The CSFs for this group were thought to be:

- prioritising potential CIs so that only those important to the business are under CMS control, and so that the most important ones are managed first;

- making sure that the size of the CMS, and effort involved in maintaining it, is appropriate to the benefits obtained;

- ensuring that CIs are appropriate to business needs and maintained in a timely manner: ensuring that accurate and up-to-date information is available to support decision-making.

The ITIL CSFs that relate to these points are:

- †"Understanding and managing the different stakeholder perspectives that underpin effective risk management within an organisation and establishing and maintaining stakeholder buy-in and commitment.

- Demonstrating that the benefits of establishing and improving the Service Transition practice and processes outweigh the costs (across the organisation and services).

- Automating processes to eliminate errors and reduce the cycle time.

- Demonstrating improved cycle time to deliver change and less variation in time, cost and quality predictions during and after transition."

No particular barriers to implementation were identified for this group.

**Business representatives**

The CSFs for this group were thought to be:

- transparent financial and cost management, with metrics, so that stakeholders can see how much value is being delivered;

- effective audit and compliance (Sarbanes–Oxley compliance was mentioned, but having an effective CMS is fundamental to many governance initiatives);

- high availability and stability ('no surprises!') and improved business continuity;

- the provision of a forward schedule of change (a forecast of changes/downtime);

- the CMS should enable potential risks to be highlighted earlier, and, ideally, pre-empted or managed.

The related ITIL CSFs are:

- †"Demonstrating that the benefits of establishing and improving the Service Transition practice and processes outweigh the costs (across the organisation and services).

- Understanding the inherent dependencies among the legacy systems, new technology and human elements that result in unknown dependencies and are risky to change.

- Demonstrating improved cycle time to deliver change and less variation in time, cost and quality predictions during and after transition.

- Automating processes to eliminate errors and reduce the cycle time.

- Being able to communicate the organisation's attitude to risk and approach to risk management more effectively during Service Transition activities.

- Building a thorough understanding of risks that have impacted or may impact the successful Service Transition of services in the Service Portfolio."

The barriers to CMS implementation for this group were thought to be:

- Poor data quality: this is typically addressed by keeping a clearly defined scope, effective configuration identification and other configuration management activities as well as aiming for close integration with other processes such as procurement, financial asset management, incident, problem and change management, and service level management;

- Budgetary constraints and resources: but a business unit that 'buys into' the CMS can partner in convincing other stakeholders to maintain commitment;

- The potential business: IT 'silo-isation', where neither side will really help the other; however, the business could help the IT group to understand the context (geographic issues, business compliance and regulations etc.) of the CMS;

- The absence of a suitable training programme: this should be planned into the initial implementation as part of an induction process and ongoing training;

- The size of the problem: which can be addressed by selecting fewer, more important CIs to manage.

### Project managers

The CSFs for this group were thought to be:

- The ability for project managers to determine what will be affected by the project based on what is there now and the ability to gauge the nature and extent of any changes;
- The ability to view what is available for reuse (hardware and software) and whether it is fit for purpose, what storage is available, licences and so on, so that it is possible to properly assess what is already available and what will need to be bought in;
- The possibility of anticipating and resolving HR issues, if the CMS holds information about people.

The related ITIL CSFs are:

- †"Understanding the inherent dependencies among the legacy systems, new technology and human elements that result in unknown dependencies and are risky to change.
- Establishing a culture that allows knowledge to be shared freely and willingly.
- Developing a workforce with the right knowledge and skills, appropriate training and the right service culture."

The barriers to CMS implementation for project managers were thought to be:

- Resistance to change and constant change: no-one likes 'being changed', especially without appropriate education and training;
- Dysfunctional cultures which may have 'fixed the audit' by hiding equipment, or may contain established fiefdoms (which will be defended to the last man), or rely on too many super heroes (one is too many) who may refuse to accept that the CMS is ever finished and who may even (apparently) steal equipment that is waiting to be deployed – overcoming this requires senior management commitment across the business, IT and customer base;
- Changing business requirements and constantly changing priorities: recognising that the data and information in the CMS will need to constantly evolve, and building in sufficient operational resources for audit and information management;
- Personality clashes: this can be managed by managing individuals, by setting clear objectives at the individual, team and organisation level and adopting organisational change methods;
- Poor baselines against which to measure CMS improvement: it is good practice to establish a base capability early in a CMS programme that enables baselines to be captured;

- Lack of CMS credibility caused by incorrect or out-of-date information in any existing configuration management system, and variable data quality generally, or poor version control, or by historical micrometric measurement of the wrong things – treat the implementation as a programme of work to establish an improved capability across the process, people and tools;
- Inconsistent terminology among the various stakeholders and lack of high-level support and coordinating vision – identify the stakeholder groups and adopt organisational and cultural change methods to focus communication and management of change at the right level.

## CONCLUSION

Kevin Holland's approach to stimulating the conference participants worked well and this is an approach that works in practice: forcing stakeholders to think about and understand the answer to challenging questions such as 'How do we stop the CMS being a mythical beast?', and to focus on the real barriers to its implementation across the relevant stakeholder groups.

Comparing the CSFs identified by the interactive stream delegates with the list in ITIL Service Transition Chapter 9, it is clear that they are broadly consistent, which is good (if nothing else, it validates ITIL as a practical, not simply a theoretical, guide).

The ITIL CSFs cover the whole of Service Transition rather than just the CMS, so you might expect them to be, in general, broader and more business and people focused, but, nevertheless, it would be useful to have a list of CSFs that are more specific to the implementation of configuration management and the CMS.

The terminology used by delegates differed to some of the ITIL terms even though many of the same issues are being addressed. This was a general issue that was raised in one of the discussions. Often this is because there are many different views from people that come from different sectors (or silos) in organisations that have achieved different levels of maturity. For some groups, such as the service desk, the delegates spoke at a more detailed level than the IITL guidance. This is probably because the service desk are daily users of the CMS and they want a CMS to support their daily activities in resolving incidents and problems, and managing requests and changes. Other stakeholder groups included CSFs from a management perspective and a user perspective.

Certain ITIL v3 'people issue' CSFs were not often mentioned in the delegate discussions and yet these CSFs should be given a lot more importance in a practical CMS implementation. These include:

- †"Developing a workforce with the right knowledge and skills, appropriate training and the right service culture.
- Defining clear accountabilities, roles and responsibilities.

- Establishing a culture that allows knowledge to be shared freely and willingly.

- Being able to appreciate and exploit the cultural and political environment.

- Developing a thorough grasp of the hard factors (processes and procedures) and soft (skills and competencies) factors required to manage a Service Transition practice."

These CSFs relate to establishing an organisational capability to manage service assets and configurations in a way that supports service management and delivers value to the business. They relate to overcoming many of the 'barriers to implementation' mentioned in the discussions. Nevertheless, they are probably more applicable to service providers that have a more mature capability in service management as well as in configuration management.

# 5 CASE STUDY OF A CMS IMPLEMENTATION

## OBJECTIVES

This chapter uses a CMDB/CMS implementation pilot to stimulate participant feedback on the issues that service providers and implementers might expect to encounter in real life.

## SUMMARY

Delegates discussed the business drivers and the incremental approach used for a pilot implementation of a CMDB/CMS in the media industry. The implementation uses a commercial toolset to support the population and maintenance of the CMDB/CMS. The organisation's reporting and monitoring capabilities, in respect of its business and IT services, improve as a result.

Delegates discussed 'What is the value and return on investment proposition for a CMDB/CMS?'. Delegates thought that maintenance of 'availability' is a key driver for the CMS, probably because of an increasing awareness of the criticality of IT for the core business. They thought that the cultural change management needed during the implementation of the CMS is of similar importance to the supporting technology.

## CMS AT ASSOCIATED NEWSPAPERS

Andrew Pieri and Mark Smith of A&N Media IT Services presented a case study for the interactive stream delegates to consider. A&N Media IT Services is a shared IT function delivering support services to Associated Newspapers Limited (ANL) and Northcliffe Media Ltd (NML), both part of Daily Mail & General Trust (DMGT), and has to deal with over 35 million print items a week and interactions with almost half of the UK population. Obviously, DMGT depends on IT to deliver its services, and 'good IT governance' is essential.

The A&N Media IT Services department has to support and deliver reliable automated services to DMGT business areas such as editorial, advertising, commercial and publishing. Within IT services, the Service Delivery group has to manage a 24/7 shift operation, with third-line support and the normal acceptance/change/problem management activities of an operations group.

The other part of IT services provides shared services for solutions management, infrastructure management and the project office.

The organisation's context for its CMS implementation is part of an overall programme to encourage 'service management thinking' into the way that IT people work. The implementation requires, as usual, a balance of people, process and technology, with due consideration of 'appropriate' best practices. ITIL practices were implemented for key processes: incident, change and problem management.

It is important to have a strategic vision behind a CMS implementation. A&N Media's vision is:

- to bring order to a fast moving, dynamic and chaotic environment;
- to move from reactive management to proactive management, and on to predictive management;
- to develop its key processes (although doing that will be a bit of a journey of discovery).

As a key part of its vision, A&N Media identifies the business benefits it expects to achieve (which are very much in line with those usually anticipated within ITIL):

- Maximise service uptime;
- Minimise risk of change;
- Take more control;
- Measure performance/set targets;
- Establish and maintain a service view of IT.

For any CMS/CMDB implementation, doing the groundwork properly is vital. Here, phase 1 of the implementation was driven by a consideration of the external organisational maturity and involved full analysis of the ITIL disciplines. A&N Media chose to focus on its existing change, incident and problem management processes with the aim of improving control, availability and the impact assessment of changes.

In an ITIL v3 context, these are covered under:

- ITIL Service Design: Availability Management;
- ITIL Service Transition: Change Management, Service Asset and Configuration Management;
- ITIL Service Operation: Incident Management, Problem Management, Event Management.

Before selecting a solution, A&N Media also identified its future requirements (an information import facility) and the capability of updating and policing configurations items.

A&N Media selected a single vendor solution with integrated support for a service desk to enhance its change and knowledge management capability. The vendor technology solution chosen enabled A&N Media to implement an operational monitoring link to the CMDB, thus enhancing its availability monitoring and reporting.

Figure 5.1 shows the implementation concept for phase 1. By underpinning the incident, problem and change management processes with a configuration management capability and CMDB, A&N Media aimed to improve the availability of operational services and enhance its capability to manage the impact of change.

**Figure 5.1** Configuration management and CMDB underpin key processes to deliver improvements

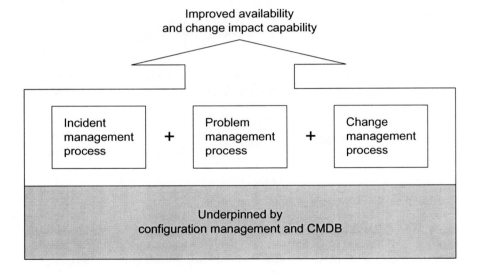

Phase 2 of the project was the actual implementation. The first implementation stage needed to be achievable to deliver real value to the business and so gain buy-in to the vision for an integrated CMS. For the A&N Media pilot, one new critical editorial service was targeted for implementation in the CMS and the scope was inclusive. The solution touched all the existing ITIL disciplines in use in the organisation for the full service architecture (i.e. all the configuration items that touched the selected editorial service). The architecture that was used for the implementation is shown in Figure 5.2.

The implementation story focused on getting the requirements right with senior management commitment. Micromanagement by top management is a bad thing for any project, but you do need to know what the organisation really wants to achieve, and senior management should be able to tell you this (if it can't, you have problems well beyond implementing a CMS).

**Figure 5.2** CMDB/CMS architecture for the case study

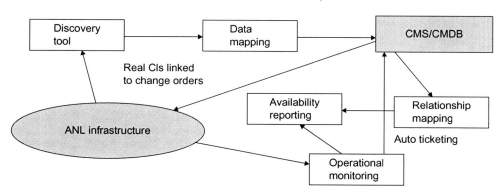

Understanding the data model underlying the CMS is important, which means understanding the semantics and structure of the assets and configurations being managed and their interrelationships. You must understand the interfaces you need to develop and establish as well as the resources you will be managing.

According to the A&N Media experience, you will meet challenges: unexpected or difficult interfaces or integrations. Most importantly, however, you must be able to recognise success (it is worthwhile blitzing success criteria before you start). In this case, success is represented by the development of:

- a facility for the configuration of new and updated CIs;
- a facility providing end-to-end metrics for availability;
- a facility offering change impact analysis;
- greater ITIL awareness, with processes matured and enhanced.

Finally, the most important part of any implementation is the lessons you learn from it. In this case, A&N Media learned that it is important to have the right resources, both internally and externally: working with the second best or whoever happens to be available does not help to guarantee success. It is also important to use an accepted framework, such as ITIL, as a resource because reinventing the wheel will not help either.

Most significantly, A&N Media learned the importance of being realistic. Integration is not easy and you should not underestimate its overheads. It learned to set realistic expectations and agree them with the appropriate stakeholders, and to pick achievable targets (such as the enablement of a single ANL service), and then to 'just start' doing it.

In addition, A&N Media learned more about what it wants to do (or needs to do, or is able to do next) during the implementation itself. Its next phase should provide reporting and impact analysis with drill-down availability reporting and hierarchical impact analysis. Then, it can develop critical services for prioritisation and choice and refine the configuration process. The chosen CMS solution should then support further process integration and fully exploit the power of the CMDB/CMS.

## CONTRIBUTORS TO THE INTERACTIVE DISCUSSION

Twenty-five contributors to the discussion represented the practitioner community. They included representatives from DeltaRail Group Limited, Mouchel, Cheshire County Council, iCore, O2, Capgemini–Aspire, NWDC, Plymouth City Council, Mentor IT Ltd., HMPS, Ericsson AB, Capgemini, ESA, Staffordshire Police, Norfolk Constabulary, Firescope Europe, Motability Operations, Fujitsu Services, Bytes and Telelogic (an IBM company).

## PARTICIPATING PRACTITIONER COMMUNITY FEEDBACK

### Associated Newspapers case study

At the start of the session, in order to provide a 'baseline' for the discussion, the A&N Media presenters asked delegates the question, 'How many organisations have used the following business drivers for your CMDB–CMS implementation?'. Working individually using the interactive technology, the delegates responded to the question by selecting from one of four options. The results were immediately displayed on the main screen for comment.

- Service Availability – 1 vote;
- Change Impact Assessment – 8 votes;
- Both – 12 votes;
- Neither – 3 votes.

Delegates were then asked whether anyone had found an integrated 'off-the-shelf solution' that supported what they were trying to do. According to the delegates, the following vendors have provided such capabilities (of course, there may be others the delegates had no experience of):

- IBM/Telelogic tools, plus CA Harvest Change Manager;
- Dimensions (Serena);
- Remedy (BMC);
- Hornbill Support Works.

Following the A&N Media presentation, the delegates were invited to give feedback on the case study via the interactive technology under the following headings:

- PLUS: This is what I liked about what I heard.
- MINUS: These are my issues and concerns.

- INTERESTING: Thoughts and insights.
- QUESTIONS: Questions for the speaker and each other.

Generally, delegates liked the clear presentation of a case study with lessons learned. Most people like the approach of starting with a single service, demonstrating improvement with a single service and building from that.

One delegate liked the 'single vendor' approach too, but another reminded people not to jump in with a service provider until you are sure that they know your business. Delegates described the A&N Media approach as 'good, sensible, pragmatic'. They were pleased to see a successful confirmatory example of such an approach from someone else, especially if it is what they would have used themselves. The comment was made that it should be easy to scale up from one service, particularly if the chosen service was typical of other services.

Delegates thought that it is significant that an incremental approach for the CMS implementation had been shown to work in an 'always on' environment. It was agreed that understanding the process was critical.

Delegates liked A&N Media's realistic honesty about the integration difficulties. However, they would have liked the case study to go into further detail about the issues with managing cultural change (that it did not is not surprising, perhaps, in a public presentation with limited time available).

After the A&N Media presentation, delegates raised various issues and concerns for CMS implementers. In particular, they thought that CMS implementers should beware of being too technology driven.

There was some discussion on whether the tools used in the case study are truly integrated and whether there are business reasons, or only technology ones, for choosing a single vendor toolset. There was also the issue of whether the tools work together 'as one' out of the box or whether there was an initial overhead in integrating them, and also whether choosing a single vendor solution might force the vendor's architecture onto the organisation. (We think that these are general issues implementers should always consider in the early stages of tool and technology selection.)

Dealing with organisational change and the people perspective was brought up as an issue. Delegates thought that there is limited published guidance relating to configuration management in this area. For instance, you may need to introduce a 'service-oriented' culture, acquire specialist skills for the software selection process, make the business case and establish key performance indicators and metrics. Implementers should think how they will get all the CMS stakeholders involved and contributing before they start. (We think that it is worth noting that the ITIL publications provide some guidance on all these aspects of managing cultural change for IT service providers.)

Delegates identified the following interesting points from the A&N Media presentation:

- Being aware of the criticality of IT for the core business and linking this to the key driver for the CMS – maintaining service 'availability'.

- Technology is by no means the whole solution.

- The incremental approach, tackling one service at a time.

- Having an overall understanding of the data captured and required by each process as well as how they will all fit together.

- Having an ITIL maturity assessment of the service provider's ability to deliver/process assessment in advance of the implementation. They liked the ITIL maturity survey, used to check progress and make it visible.

- Establishing the business case by delivering higher availability through improvements to the incident, problem and change management processes. The CMS is seen as 'merely' being an enabler for achieving these business benefits.

A range of general questions were raised by the delegates. These are summarised in the points below and we have provided commentary and references to the chapters in this book where they are covered, if appropriate:

- Identifying and quantifying the benefits and agreeing the success criteria and identifying the right Key Performance Indicators (KPIs), ideally at the business level.

    o This is covered in Chapter 4 and Chapter 12. After implementation, you must be able to show that you were successful. Documenting a pre-implementation baseline (such as the ITIL maturity assessment) is an important aspect of this. You should try to identify specific benefits (e.g. reduced outage) and check that they been achieved after implementation.

- One issue identified by the CMS implementers in the discussion group, who are generally CMS enthusiasts, is that 'heroic' change management (depending on a key 'change hero' who just makes change happen) can be popular with general (non-specialist) developers and their managers. It can appear to be very successful for managing changes in the short term, at least, and the 'heroes' can be popular figures, which makes gaining commitment to a CMS more difficult.

    o In our experience, reliance on 'change heroes' comes with significant, often un-assessed, risk and does not address the wider CMS issue, but we do recognise that it can make showing the benefits from moving to an institutionalised CMS process (i.e. a CMS process embedded in the organisation's culture: see Appendix 1) harder. Addressing this issue requires investment in managing cultural change and CMS awareness, possibly using charismatic 'CMS champions', possibly brought in from outside.

- Identification of the business drivers. For example, if 'availability' is important, it should map onto a business case.

  o Our experience is that an ITIL gap analysis helps to get people started, but that you should not use ITIL for its own sake. It is vital to link the CMS implementation to business benefit (direct or indirect) as demonstrated in this case study.

- Tools for the CMDB and discovery of configurations concerned delegates (see Chapter 9). One question was about the application of discovery tools to maintain the configuration information. For example, once you have captured legacy data using discovery tools, do you use the discovery tool again to keep it up to date, or do you rely on the change management process to keep the information current, going forward?

  o In our experience, sometimes organisations rely on the change and configuration management process to keep the information updated and sometimes a combination of the process and a discovery tool is used. For example, the process identifies that a change is made and the discovery tool establishes the configuration baseline before and after the change. A discovery tool is useful when auditing and verifying the data in the CMS. There is an issue if the automated discovery and monitoring tools do not fully support a service view.

- Do you have to compromise your requirements in order to implement a single vendor solution, and, if so, is this a good idea?

  o We think that the work involved in customising a single vendor solution must be considered as this affects the business case. For example, does data mapping involve handcrafted scripting or out-of-the-box functionality from the discovery tool vendor? These are important questions to consider during the design of a CMS solution. (See Chapter 9 and the ITIL Service Design volume.)

- Managing capacity with respect to the CMS implementation.

  o We think that the scope and size of the resources required to operate the CMS and supporting organisation or function are important considerations in the business case. For example, how many configuration items (CIs) do you expect, and how many requests for change against those CIs? What size of configuration management team do you need? The ITIL Service Design publication provides guidance on capacity management.

- Implementing organisational and cultural change. Will implementers need to ensure that the cultural change associated with CMS implementation keeps pace with the technical change?

  o We think that organisations will need to manage an organisational change programme in parallel with the technical implementation and ensure that all stakeholders are involved. Jobs/roles may need defining/redefining for the new processes. This is an organisational issue, so you should get the HR department involved. Process and technology training for the CMS users is important (see Chapter 11). The ITIL Service Transition publication provides guidance on organisational and cultural change as well as guidance on implementing a CMS.

- The viability of the incremental approach. How does this approach work without certain key facilities being already in place? For example, starting with incident, problem and change management is fine, but how do you ensure that data is accurate without including release management?

    o We think that the best answer to this real issue is that you should plan and design or model the whole CMS service before planning the (incremental) physical implementation of part of it, and make sure that the implementation copes with any missing parts of the whole (see Chapter 10).

## CONCLUSION

A CMDB/CMS enables a service provider to plan and manage changes to its services and configurations. Andrew Pieri and Mark Smith of A&N Media presented a good case study of how to implement configuration management in practice.

Reporting the availability of an end-to-end service requires an understanding of the business usage and impact of the service as well as the underlying technology configurations. A&N Media's vision statements are clear and easy for people to understand, especially since they have started to implement the ITIL service management processes. In this setting, it is relatively easy for people to understand the importance of configuration management and the need for accurate configuration information. The cultural change to 'service management thinking' helped A&N Media to keep the right focus on the business and supporting technology services.

A&N Media selected a single vendor solution with integrated support for a service desk to enhance its change and knowledge management capability. A contributing factor to selecting this technology solution is the ability to implement an operational monitoring link to the CMDB to enhance availability monitoring and reporting in the future. Although there are some risks in selecting a single vendor solution as opposed to 'best of breed', there can be fewer consequent issues in developing an integrated CMS. Knowing the overall business and IT requirements should help an organisation to select the right product(s).

The A&N Media approach described in the case study works well, probably for the following reasons:

- Aiming to establish the basic controls for a business critical service to improve availability represents good governance and is usually supported by both business and IT managers.

- Clear sponsorship and management of the work as a project ensures continued commitment to delivering real business benefit.

- Building on the existing acceptance, change, incident and problem management process activities makes sense to people. This helps with the cultural change.

- Demonstrating that configuration management can be used to support the service management of an end-to-end service reinforces a cultural shift to 'service management thinking'.

- Selecting a business critical service helps to get commitment. It enables an organisation to start to demonstrate adherence to a variety of regulations and minimises corporate risk. It is hard for anyone to argue that business critical services and their configurations should not be controlled.

- A new service is an obvious point to capture configuration information. It creates a sense of urgency for the completion of information capture during the initial build, release and deployment.

- Implementation of a new service ensures that the corresponding configuration and data models are designed into the overall solution for the new service.

- Using an inclusive approach to capturing all configuration items for a new service helps to define a good CMS architecture and configuration data model that will enable better control of an organisation's assets and configurations.

- Providing the knowledge and information to do better impact analysis of changes, incidents and problems affects many people and this helps to embed (institutionalise) configuration management into the accepted ways of working.

- Integrating the incident, problem and change management processes with configuration management with the CMDB enables an organisation to demonstrate improvements in the availability of an end-to-end service.

A&N Media's business case for implementing a CMDB/CMS solution is centred on improving service availability levels and the impact assessment of changes. This case study shows that a CMDB/CMS can overcome real challenges in maintaining and changing services, assets and configurations. Establishing basic controls reduces the number of incorrectly configured assets that cause variation in service availability and unsuccessful changes that result in incidents impacting the business and few will argue that this isn't a good thing.

# 6 HOW TO IMPROVE AN EXISTING CONFIGURATION MANAGEMENT PROCESS

## OBJECTIVES

The objectives of this chapter are to add to the existing body of knowledge around identifying and addressing configuration management failures and to use this to improve the configuration management process.

## SUMMARY

To improve a configuration management process, you first have to recognise that something is wrong and assess the existing process. This assessment should provide a baseline that any process improvements can be measured against. This chapter explains that the essential foundation for improvement is a body of engaged stakeholders that are involved with the process and contribute to the improvement process. Improvements are best achieved by addressing specific pain points, so this chapter also documents likely configuration management pain points.

## HOW TO IMPROVE AN EXISTING CM PROCESS

John Metcalfe (of BCS CMSG) and Deirdre Connis (of itSMF CCRM) found that previous CMSG and itSMF events provided a useful body of knowledge around how CM practitioners can recognise that something is going wrong with the process and how to improve it. This body of knowledge provides possible options for dealing with CM process issues. Some of these were presented to stimulate the interactive discussion.

For example, the classic symptom of a poor CM process is that the organisation loses all control over the status or location of its assets: objects 'disappear' when you move between environments, people are testing the wrong versions of system components, bugs that have been fixed suddenly reappear, the wrong version of a system or component appears in production, and various environments run out of free disk space. This last symptom is an interesting one, because at first glance it can look like a user problem (people simply are not managing their disk space), but what if the system locks up as a consequence of users inadvertently deleting important files? Users' reluctance to tidy up their own disk space can sometimes be a rational response to the failure of configuration management: when an organisation does not know where important assets are and what status they are in, deleting anything could be high risk. So, lack of disk space can sometimes be merely a symptom of a bigger problem.[1]

The lesson here is that you must beware of and analyse the unintended consequences from apparently sensible actions when processes aren't working well. When configuration management is failing you may see a variety of symptoms resulting from a range of apparently fairly sensible actions (such as tidying up disk space and code libraries) but it is important to identify the fundamental root cause of all of these symptoms, not merely their many immediate causes, if you want to improve the CM process. You should start by prioritising and deploying suitable techniques for detecting failure, but then you must subject these failure reports to some form of root cause analysis.

Once you have determined that you have CM issues that need to be resolved, the next stage is to establish the key stakeholders in the improvement process. Then, one way to actively engage these stakeholders in the improvement process is to address specific pain points. For example you could look at recent failures. If connecting a router to a rack in the wrong computer room has brought down the data centre, for example, you should investigate whether this is a one-off mistake or whether the root cause is a faulty process. If the latter, then you should revise the process with the help of the affected stakeholders, and publicise the improvement. This not only reduces the risk of this failure happening again, but also publicises the benefits from process improvement.

Key approaches to supporting and promoting CM improvement are:

- using routine process monitoring to ensure that you know that something is going wrong;

- capturing user feedback on the existing process and reviewing incidents as they are addressed, so that lessons can be learnt from them;

- using regular formal audits to identify issues, risks and discrepancies (between, for example, the operational world and the CMDB);

- encouraging stakeholder sponsorship through presenting a business case for any improvement and by addressing the specific business-level pain points these stakeholders experience;

- engaging stakeholders by actively publicising and 'selling' the business and other benefits of process improvement and by inviting stakeholders to contribute to the improvement process;

- making sure that you know configuration information actually used in anger is maintained and that you know who is really responsible for its completeness and accuracy.

### The initial presentation summarised

According to Metcalfe and Connis, as well as using existing process improvement methods, there are several generic 'rules of thumb' from the existing body of knowledge that you should take account of when undertaking process improvement:

- Configuration management must establish friendly and effective working relationships with all impacted parties within the programme.[2]
- Affordable solutions that work for four people lead to problems for larger teams.[3]
- Never forget the importance of 'ownership' for a CM solution.[3]
- You should consider the established Capability Maturity Model (CMM) goals for software configuration management:

  o Software work products are identified, controlled and available.

  o Configuration management activities are planned.

  o Changes to identified work products are controlled.

  o Affected groups are informed of the status and content of software baselines.[4]

## CONTRIBUTORS TO THE INTERACTIVE SESSION

Twenty-four contributors to the discussion represented the practitioner community. They included representatives from BAE Systems, Associated Newspapers, ESA, Fujitsu Services, Virgin Media TV, itSMF UK, Cheshire Police, Financial Times, Met Office, GSK, Plymouth City Council, Cargill PLC, TATA Consultancy Services, Tsystems, Atos Origin, Allen & Overy, DHL IS Europe, Hornbill and Bytes technology group.

## PARTICIPATING PRACTITIONER COMMUNITY FEEDBACK

### What techniques/processes do you have in place to detect failures?
The delegates were asked to consider and discuss examples of the CM process failures based on the feedback from previous workshops and then to document the techniques and processes they had in place to detect or highlight failure. Techniques for detecting failure were grouped under nine headings:

- Monitoring and control;
- Auditing;
- Testing;
- Incident and defect management;
- Problem management;
- Change management;
- Automation and tools;
- Lifecycle controls;
- Culture and organisation.

Frequently, delegates went on to add suggestions for resolving detected failures. For example they thought that 'controls' help to detect, anticipate or mitigate failure, as well as helping to identify improvements.

## Monitoring and control

Delegates thought that the key to identifying CM problems proactively is to implement good monitoring and control processes supported by tools. For example generating exception reports against early warning thresholds is useful. Delegates pointed out that formal controls should be enforced if they are to improve the reliability of the CM process. If you design controls properly they should highlight failures for exception reporting to management. At the very least, delegates said that 'you'll need to be able "lock down" who can "push the buttons" and release to the production environment'.

We would point out that often when organisations try to do this, informal change paths will be highlighted because people complain that the controls prevent them from doing something they need to do. You should be careful to ensure that new controls are implemented via change management and introduced first in 'reporting mode' (or they could cause a production failure).

Delegates suggested that the following monitoring techniques are known to work in practice:

- Monitoring KPIs and measurements. Delegates said that you should 'identify correct KPIs like uptime, and monitor performance against KPIs. Reassess KPIs if one is always failing – look for the root cause.' However, delegates also pointed out that you need to be careful to 'detect non-workable conditions like impossible KPIs'.

- Using monitoring tools with thresholds set to provide early warnings (e.g. threshold levels set to detect failure against an SLA before it becomes critical).

- Using a wide range of monitoring techniques and activities instead of just monitoring one or two things:

  o Operational monitoring;

  o Production monitoring (i.e. identify where we expect to be, against where we are not getting what we expected, indicating possible errors);

  o Application performance monitoring;

  o End-to-end availability monitoring;

  o Monitoring lack of capacity;

  o System and server monitoring (e.g. to identify 'hot spots' where servers are getting near capacity).

We think that these techniques can apply to monitoring a business outcome (or business KPI), an overall service, an environment or part of a system, product or service and that many of these may be interconnected. In the case of a failure being reported against an SLA, for example, the root cause could be that operations management is unable to maintain service quality in the current architecture or that there are insufficient resources to deliver the required service level targets. The failure could also be caused by a badly configured asset or a process failure and so monitoring at the asset or process level would be useful.

We think good KPIs provide a strong basis for monitoring and that capacity reports and capacity threshold warnings can be particularly useful as they often provide an early indication of potential service or assets failure due to lack of capacity.

### Auditing

Delegates identified techniques for auditing configurations, environments and processes either by auditors, procedures and/or automation. These were:

- generic audit and verification procedures, including discovery techniques;

- auditing via a discovery engine as a specific technique;

- the use of internal and external auditors;

- auditing the full estate (people, processes, tools and equipment), identifying non-conformances, looking for root causes where a full audit can be justified by regulatory or other high-profile requirements;

- an audit of part of the estate, often carried out as part of a review of a major incident for a business critical service to see if the root cause is related to change and/or configuration management;

- auditing build processes regularly and reviewing build logs to provide confidence that a system, product or service is correctly configured at the time it is created.

Delegates suggested that automated audits via a discovery engine may be easier to manage than manual audits.

However, we'd point out that that automated discovery has limitations. In some environments, key systems may not be connected to the network for security reasons, and sometimes obsolescent machines or legacy environments cannot support the agents some discovery engines need. Also, automated audits cannot cover certain types of configuration items such as business services and rules.

We do think that auditors can be a good source of information about failing processes because they are professional, independent and taken seriously by management. On the other hand, auditors can annoy people, for example if they are not technically aware or if an audit is conducted too early when the process is not established.

### Testing

Testing was specifically mentioned by delegates as helping to identify and highlight CM failures (both pre-production defects and production incidents). Delegates recommended:

- testing that looks for specific problem fixes that have been incorporated into the release, with every subsequent release including this test in its test suite;

- extensive automated testing from pre-release through to production;
- regression testing;
- testing done by an independent testing function that signs off fitness for release to the production environment;
- testing on reference environments (check that a test configuration is appropriate);
- testing procedures used to test the code before release to the live environment.

### Incident and defect management

Delegates identified the following techniques and activities as assisting with failure detection:

- Defect management: covering pre-production and production environments.
- Help desk/service desk: providing a single point of contact for customer/users.
- Getting customers to report where they are having troubles when they occur, rather than just complaining to each other.
- Incident management: with regular meetings to discuss and prioritise actions to change operating practices and procedures, particularly after critical or major incidents.
- Incident and problem management: detecting and recording all service outages and known errors, and relating back to the service catalogue for impact analysis.
- Defect and incident management of pre-production and production environments.
- User/customer feedback and complaints: helping to detect process failures and failures in management processes can also highlight impossible conditions, such as infeasible KPIs.

We agree that seeking cooperation from interested stakeholders both inside and outside the IT community helps to identify issues. It also helps if a service provider logs all defects and incidents because this provides historical records that can be analysed to identify root causes of failure, potential risks and areas for improvement.

### Problem management

Several delegates suggested using problem management process and techniques as follows:

- Problem management: looking for recurring issues.
- Trending on issues that regularly occur to ensure that they can be resolved prior to another failure.
- Proactive problem management.
- Error detection.

We would point out that problem management is an accepted ITIL process that has the objectives of preventing incidents from happening, and minimising the impact of incidents that cannot be prevented. Proactive problem management is used to identify problems that might otherwise be missed, by analysing incident records, and using data collected by other IT service management processes in order to identify trends or significant general problems.

### Change management
Delegates identified the following activities in change management for detecting or highlighting process failure:

- Documenting evidence of people bypassing the change control process, together with the tracking and reporting of authorised changes.

- Management enforcement of a robust change process, supported by tools that compare the live estate with the most recent baseline or stable state.

- Rigorous change control and change management processes with effective risk and impact analysis.

- Implementation of a forward schedule of change.

We think that the ability of an organisation to enforce the change management process depends on good management of the configurations and vice versa. Tracking and reporting unauthorised changes depends on the capability and maturity of the organisation and the processes for incident, problem, change, configuration and release management and audit. Many organisations have a change management policy that requires all parties to adopt the change management process.

However, in our experience, detecting unauthorised changes for many services and environments can be very difficult unless there are tight controls, good audit processes and tools with supporting processes. Some organisations that have implemented incident and problem management processes do at least start to detect incidents caused by unauthorised changes.

Again, our experience is that using a forward schedule of changes enables an organisation to identify potential clashes that could impact service and IT configurations in advance. Many organisations deliver significant improvements by implementing a forward schedule of changes supported by their change and configuration management processes.

### Automation and tools
Several delegates identified automation as a way of improving configuration management to support the other techniques in this chapter. The techniques they recommended were:

- automated alert systems and dashboards;

- automatic builds from controlled access libraries;

- automatic build after checking early warning of compilation errors during the development stage in the lifecycle;

- automatic testing for consistent testing;
- use of source code management system that provides a configuration baseline for each release.

Within the context of configuration management, delegates thought that automation helps to:

- automatically detect errors;
- reduce human errors;
- reduce the cost of repetitive jobs such as build and audit;
- check access control quickly and efficiently;
- detect errors early in the lifecycle;
- get the right information to the right people at the right time to validate an activity or make a decision.

We agree that automation can enable configuration management improvement, but would emphasise that automation alone is not sufficient. The overall solution will also require improvements in process and people's capabilities.

### Lifecycle controls

Delegates thought that the development lifecycle as a whole, and the CM lifecycle stages in particular, provide controls that help to identify failure and correct failures:

- Defining roles and responsibilities across the lifecycle helps to allocate clear responsibilities and this helps in highlighting process failure.
- A design and code compliance matrix helps to identify requirements you are failing to satisfy.
- Gathering requirements in the early stages of a project and prioritising these requirements helps to highlight failures later on.

We agree that it is important to take a holistic approach to failure and to look at the whole lifecycle – remember that failure in your CM processes only really matters of it impacts the delivery of an automated service to the business.

### Culture and organisation

Some delegates mentioned the importance of cultural and organisational maturity issues:

- They pointed out that 'controlling developers is extremely difficult'.
- Some delegates employed lean techniques: process mapping, gap analysis, value stream improvements and so on.

We'd point out that when you start thinking about improving configuration management you'll worry about the technology issues, but if it all goes wrong it will probably be because of people issues. We agree that controlling developer creative free spirits can be hard.

We think that the IT culture in an organisation should be configuration management aware (you can achieve this through training) and that then identifying CM failures won't be the sole responsibility of the CM team (so long as the organisational structure and culture supports feedback of such information to the CM team). In a dysfunctional organisation, a computer operator, say, who highlights an impending CMS failure might be thought of as a 'troublemaker', which will not help the cause of CMS improvement.

We agree that a CMS-friendly organisational culture might well employ 'lean' techniques. However, it might also simply implement operational good practice, such as system and server monitoring to identify 'hot spots' where servers are getting near capacity. Even implementing an effective software lifecycle development process should help the cause of configuration management improvement (it gives you a process to work with).

As far as organisational structure goes, we think that quality assurance (QA), testing and configuration management should report into the business in parallel with development and deployment management. Otherwise conflicts of interest can lead to CM failures being hidden.

### Techniques/processes to resolve problems/improve configuration management
Next, delegates were invited to suggest ways in which they might resolve problems and correct shortcomings in practice. The feedback for this was grouped under three headings:

- Process (including the controls suggested in the previous section);
- Reviews;
- Tools.

### Process
Delegates said that they use enforcement of their controls in their processes; one said, 'you'll need to be able "lock down" who can "push the buttons" and release to the production environment'.

They would implement a forward schedule of change, proactive problem management and critical incident management with regular meetings to discuss and prioritise improvement actions. They tried to build in-house automation for support departments with the same attention to the analysis as would be given to a business system and they needed a 'defined, documented process, with the "hand-offs" made clear'.

The process delegates suggested using provides for:

- a physical technology model (PTM), as well as a logical technology model;
- configuration audits;

- equipment assessment and replacement of failing units;
- the opportunity for consultation with industry experts;
- automated discovery, used to ensure data accuracy for lower level attributes on CIs;
- a process for communicating inconsistencies with CI data to the stakeholders owning it;
- a process for the publication of data (good and bad).

Delegates wanted 'defined roles and responsibilities with delegated and acknowledged ownership'. In return, stakeholders can expect weekly status reports, such as major incident reports or CI status reports to help them fulfil their responsibilities.

Delegates wanted their process to include the ability to 'track back release records to the service catalogue, application and infrastructure' and to verify the accuracy of the CMDB content. They can 'compare database and systems and align them if needed'. Rigorous change control, continuous process assessment, and functional and physical audits of CIs, processes, tools and databases are all thought to be important. One delegate pointed out that the CMS itself must be subject to configuration management, with 'change requests and approval for inconsistencies or changes to be made in the CMDB'.

Delegates made the service owner 'accountable for the corresponding CIs and their relationships' and provided training to institutionalise process. Subsequently, the improved process should not be optional, however, it should provide a way for someone to do things better than the current process (so long as it doesn't have undesirable repercussions for anyone else), with a controlled way for the process to change so as to accommodate this innovation.

That, after all, is what CMS improvement is, and it needn't always come from the CMS team. As a delegate said, 'we use [the] knowledge of [the] working team to trigger suggestions and improvements'.

### Reviews
Reviews are a specific part of process, of course, but worthwhile highlighting in their own right. One of the most useful reviews delegates used is the post-implementation review (PIR): a 'check on all changes: that what was implemented matches what the change said it was'.

We point out that, unfortunately, this is the review least likely to be implemented in an immature organisation with an active 'blame culture'.

Delegates said that audit and verification processes and procedures are necessary and used the following reviews:

- Regular review of process, issues and status with users and customers (perhaps 'a mandatory six-month review of process').
- Auditing for capability and maturity 'to ensure maintenance of uniformity of application'.

- Review of expected outcomes against actual outcomes: 'Did the CM system deliver? Did we encounter the problems we thought we would?'

Delegates considered audits to be a kind of review. Audit reports can show when key pieces of information are missing in the database: the minimum requirements for input of a CI can be determined and then escalated back to the originating team if all information is not available. An audit can be a benchmark against established good practice.

Each CI record is owned by a stakeholder (possibly in the IT department) who is responsible for the updates to it. When an audit is then undertaken (using discovery tools and similar) and something is missing or has changed, then the responsible individual or team is notified so that they can update the record.

In our experience, open user forums or special interest groups can be formed to share knowledge and if a confidential reporting line is available, on which people can leave anonymous 'tip-offs' concerning potential or actual issues, the people at the sharp end (who generally know all too well what is going wrong) can be part of the review process. However, anonymous feedback should always be independently verified before acting on it.

### Tools
Delegates made the point that, although tools are important for enabling CM improvement, some tools are better than others. Tools are regularly assessed (tools that aren't being used indicate that something is wrong) and problems with them corrected (we'd note that you mustn't overlook the importance of training). Where it is possible, automation is used to ensure consistency and reduce the opportunity for user error; delegates mention using source code management systems, using deployment tools in order to remove or reduce manual interactions and using CM agents running on servers and reporting back to a central point.

We agree that automated, agent-based, configuration management enables automatic alignment to a service, so if something has appeared against a service overnight, for example, then it will appear in an exception report that can be checked against change records. However, do be aware of the limitations of such agents (e.g. they may not run on all platforms).

### CONCLUSION

This session highlighted the role of measurement, monitoring and control in order to ensure that a system, product, process or service is configured correctly, and/or that it functions exactly as specified. Our experience tells us that appropriate measures and controls should be clearly defined, executed and acted on across the software, systems and service lifecycle.

Many of the techniques suggested by delegates are processes that enable detection of configuration, CMS or process failures, including techniques for:

- monitoring and control;
- defect and incident management;
- problem management (reactive and proactive);
- change and configuration management;
- testing;
- audit.

Correctly identifying the root causes behind the (often) many symptoms of failure is, we think, an important critical success factor. Delegates pointed out that once the root cause of failure is identified and understood, what actions to take are usually fairly obvious.

We note that the feedback from this interactive session is fairly unstructured by its very nature. In sorting and ordering the responses, it is clear that many of the techniques suggested do, in fact, come from other processes within the systems development lifecycle and IT service management generally. Specifically, many of them already exist within ITIL, often outside configuration management. ITIL should be used as a resource in order to avoid reinventing the wheel. We also note that practitioners did not really distinguish between the process of detecting failure and the processes of analysing and addressing failures: they appeared to see all of these as aspects of one process. Separating these out and analysing the root cause of failure could lead to better investment in improvements that deliver significant business benefits.

The interactive session behind this chapter reinforced the need for CM practitioners not to operate in a configuration management silo and to make use of other processes, where appropriate, in their pursuit of continual improvement.

# 7 SERVICE MANAGEMENT REQUIREMENTS FOR A CMDB/CMS

**OBJECTIVES**

The objectives of this chapter are to present an approach to determining the service management requirements for a CMDB/CMS and to identify the common requirements for service management met in practice.

**SUMMARY**

A wide range of stakeholders across an organisation have requirements for the CMS and these requirements should be gathered from all of them. It is suggested that a requirements clarification approach, built around structured use case workshops, will be most fruitful. A list of generic requirements is provided and the issues around gathering requirements are discussed.

**SERVICE MANAGEMENT REQUIREMENTS FOR A CMDB/CMS**

The ITIL Service Design volume defines requirements as †"a formal statement of what is needed": in this case for a specific organisation's CMS. Chapter 3 of the volume, Service Design Principles, documents the means for identifying service requirements (Section 3.3) and emphasises the importance of a holistic approach. Section 3.4 covers the identification and documentation of business requirements and drivers. Section 5.1 describes requirements engineering in general, which is equally applicable to the design of CMS services. These sections provide a very useful complement to this chapter.

Ian Salvage (then Service Management Consultant, IBM Global Services) told the interactive stream delegates about the importance of gathering requirements from all the stakeholders in the CMS, across the full breadth of IT and (possibly) user management, as well as any 'actors' in any of the organisation's service management processes. In one engagement, he had reached out to representatives of specific users (although the representatives were still within IT) and found it a useful exercise, although the sessions turned into more of an education session on what configuration management was, because the representatives were not sufficiently primed in advance.

He emphasised the need for a strong foundation for requirements gathering. You need to discover the top-down vision for what the CMS should deliver, by looking at:

- organisational or departmental mission statements;
- any vision statements;
- documentation of future goals;
- any published guiding principles for the organisation.

You will also need to address the governance issues around implementing the CMS by identifying the appropriate CSFs (see Chapter 4) and agreeing success criteria (the objective measurements of success) for the CMS implementation project. You should also agree the basis for making strategic decisions during the life of the project, identify any assumptions you are making and agree the project's scope.

You will also need to define a framework within which the CMS solution can be defined clearly. This framework will need to consider:

- any guiding principles for configuration management, perhaps based on those in the ITIL volumes;
- regulatory or compliance requirements, including any specific, identified audit deficiencies that need remediation;
- common audit or certification requirements, taken from accepted industry 'good practice';
- any existing process models or frameworks adopted by your organisation;
- applicable standards, whether international (such as ISO 10007:2003 for *Quality management systems – Guidelines for configuration management*, and ISO/IEC 20000 for Service Management) or national, vendor, industry-based or organisational standards;
- security requirements, for the confidentiality, integrity or availability of the CMS service or its data (and do not overlook integration with the organisation identity management systems, if it has any);
- any other organisational systems, programmes or projects that might impact the CM requirements and the CMS.

Only after you have determined the scope and framework for your requirements gathering can you be sure of gathering the requirements effectively. It is important to realise that configuration management only exists to provide information that will support other processes, so you will need to know what information these other processes require. A good way to do this is with a use case workshop for each process the CMS needs to support, using use cases to identify the requirements of the interfacing processes.

Use case modelling was originated by Ivar Jacobson in the late 1980s. A use case describes 'who' can do 'what' with the system in question, which is the CMS in the present case. It describes the system from the user's point of view and the interaction between one or more actors and the system itself, represented as a sequence of simple steps. Actors may exist outside the CMS and take part in a sequence of activities in a dialogue with the system to achieve some goal (e.g. to identify the IT financial assets for the finance department). Actors may be end users, other systems or devices. Many organisations will have in-house expertise with use cases in the systems development group and many books describe their uses (e.g. *Use Case Modelling* by Kurt Bittner and Ian Spence, with a foreword by Ivar Jacobson, ISBN 978-0-201709-13-1).

Use cases provide a structured approach to identifying the key interfaces, data requirements and roles associated with an activity. Each use case has a name, a list of the actors involved in it and their relationships. The use case will identify:

- an initiating actor;
- whatever triggers the use case;
- its data requirement, including the data source, configuration item type and relationships;
- any supporting use cases or preconditions;
- its termination outcomes.

An example of a use case was presented for the 'assess change' process. The activities in the given process, together with the contents of the use case, were used as the basis for a workshop discussion. The data collated during the use case workshops provided the link between the strategic drivers and requirements and the specific CM requirements: CI types, attributes, relationships, data sources, functional requirements, process interfaces, organisational information, enablers and inhibitors.

After this presentation, the assembled delegates were asked to discuss the approach to defining the requirements from their respective points of view.

## CONTRIBUTORS TO THE INTERACTIVE SESSION

Thirteen contributors to the discussion represented the practitioner community. They included representatives from Teliasonera, EDS, O2, Telelogic (an IBM company), Unilever, DeltaRail, Fujitsu Services, TfL, EADS DS UK Ltd and Lea-Cox Associates.

## PARTICIPATING PRACTITIONER COMMUNITY FEEDBACK

Delegates were asked at the start of this interactive session to consider what the key generic service management requirements for the CMDB/CMS solution might be. Their answers were:

- It should be possible to discover what is in use in the organisation quickly, which means that the CMS must be updated and verified efficiently and regularly.
- Service management and services:
    - What is the organisation's policy/strategy for service management?
    - Who are the service management process owners?

- o What service management infrastructure do we require?
- o What services are we going to manage?
- o Who are the service stakeholders?

- Decision support and reporting:

  - o It should hold the kinds of data needed for decision support.
  - o It should provide accurate reports in a timely fashion, for impact assessment and analysis, and for supporting management decisions.
  - o It should be able to query the data and create ad hoc reports.
  - o Reports should be straightforward to interpret.
  - o Ad hoc reporting should be possible.

- Information and data:

  - o Who owns the data?
  - o Who should be allowed to see and/or update the data?
  - o It should be easy to access for the right people and restricted where appropriate.
  - o It should be trustworthy.
  - o It should be available in a timely manner.
  - o It should provide facilities to collate and relate data.
  - o It should provide accurate (correct, trusted) information in a timely manner.

- Change management:

  - o The CMS should include changes and support the CM process.

We note that, in order to be useful, specific requirements must be 'testable'. In other words, requirements for a CMS must be defined well enough for the implementers of the CMS to decide whether the CMS, in fact, implements them.

Following the presentation, delegates were invited to give feedback via the interactive technology.

**This is what I liked about what I heard**
Delegate feedback suggested that the idea of requirements workshops for the CMS/CMDB from business need was generally liked. The feedback obtained was that the following aspects of the approach are specifically liked:

- Practical: 'examples of use cases for specific functionality'.
- 'The sound and sensible approach.'
- 'The coordinated approach to structuring the CMS/CMDB.'

- The 'logical structure', although the availability of a description of the overall approach was questioned.
- 'The concept of being able to structure the development of the CMS as a manageable project, this presentation gives practical suggestions on how to do that.'
- 'The idea of work-shopping the requirements for CMDB, being driven from business need.'
- 'The good introduction to the lifecycle and V-model for the CMDB/CMS.'

### Issues, concerns, thoughts and insights

The following issues, concerns, thoughts and insights were identified:

- 'For extant systems that are already under resourced it would be extremely difficult to get the required buy-in and commitment from management and staff for this type of approach.'
- 'Really [this is] talking about the architecture of the CMDB and CMS – this is more than just requirements.'
- 'CMDBs cost money. They don't come free.'
- 'Need additional skill sets to do analysis – who may be focused on software and not service management.'
- 'Not only [should you] involve configuration managers and service managers but [you should] include in the implementation approach also skills such as information analysts and information architects.'
- 'Making the generic use cases available may prove to be useful.'

We think that the need for commitment from management and staff has been covered in other sessions (See Chapters 3 and 4). Obtaining people with the right skills for the use case workshops and analysis is often an issue, but identifying the need at the start of a project will help. The design of the CMS/CMDB architecture should be considered as part of the high-level requirements.

We agree that a key issue for many organisations can be obtaining up front the funding to define the overall architecture of the CMDB/CMS and appropriate CMS applications and tools. This is particularly so if an evolutionary approach to implementing configuration management is adopted. However, with this type of approach it is even more important that the CMS/CMDB architecture is considered early.

We also agree that, because the CMS provides the information and data for service management, projects that design and implement the CMS should include information architects and analysts as well as the service owners, process owners and managers within service management, change and configuration management.

We think that the possibility of sharing generic use cases within the industry is useful but note that delegates also said that there will be business-specific use cases for each organisation.

**Questions for the speaker and each other**

The questions raised in the session were grouped together with our responses.

- Are metadata requirements from the wider organisation important?

  o There are often metadata requirements from the wider organisation and this is why it is important to include all stakeholders. Examples include procurement, financial asset management and business operations.

- There are requirements to populate the CMDB and requirements that the service management disciplines have of the CMDB. Should these be done at the same time? Are CI types requirements or are they solutions to business requirements?

  o The requirements should be considered at the same time. Otherwise updating the CMDB will not meet the stakeholder requirements during implementation. Configuration identification is the business activity that defines the scope of configuration management (usually phased), the CI types, naming standards and relationships between CIs and other records (change, problem, incident records) and this forms part of the requirements.

- When other process requirements are identified, does there need to be a push back from CMDB to ensure data ownership and maintenance?

  o When other process and data requirements are identified, they should be owned by a specific role, for example the CIO, appropriate process owners/managers and service owners/managers. These requirements should link into the organisation's vision, overall service management requirements and business case for the CMS at each phase of implementation. By doing this, requirements can be prioritised across different stakeholders. Chapter 5 provides an example of a pilot of an implementation for one service that supports service level management, availability management and change management. The scope of this pilot was clear to the organisation and there was ownership of the relevant processes and service. It is better to set clear principles for configuration management, data ownership and maintenance and have a clear implementation strategy, then you can be seen to be prioritising within the overall principles and strategy rather than being seen to 'push back'. However, if you have to 'push back', you can do so within a clear scope and set of rules.

- Are use cases a generic format used across the industry or are they created in-house to be business specific?

  o Use cases can be generic where there is standardisation across the industry. For example generic use cases for impact analysis by incident management, problem management and change management can be based on the ITIL practices. Often a generic use case will need to be modified for an organisation, especially when other disciplines outside IT are involved. One example is where there is an organisational interface such as between financial asset management and configuration management.

- I think this approach is based on rational unified process (RUP), which is traditionally software. How can you sell this approach to service management and operations who are usually more product/PRINCE focused?

  - It is often best to use the organisation's existing approach to gathering and defining the requirements because there will be supporting tools, processes and people with relevant skills in the organisation.

- What other techniques are effective for finding service management-related requirements? How effective are use cases compared with other methods?

  - The traditional approach is to use more-or-less structured interviewing of key stakeholders. Traditional techniques, however, have issues with user involvement and even with getting the right people to interview. A use case workshop is more likely to get people involved.

- How do you obtain buy-in from clients when discussing and agreeing requirements/design?

  - A workshop approach and use cases do work if the focus of the requirements is based on business needs and linked to service management requirements. Use cases help to keep the focus at the right level, for example using the CMS to deliver a process outcome rather than defining low-level functional requirements.

- What are the repeating themes that come from the workshops?

  - Each workshop tends to have a specific focus. Example workshops might be incident and problem management, change and release management, service design, financial and asset management, capacity and availability management, energy usage management. Therefore, each is likely to result in different functional requirements for the CMS. Common themes are driven more by the framework within which the CMS solution can be defined clearly, as mentioned earlier in this chapter.

- Is this a standard approach that IBM takes when considering service management/CMS requirements? Or is it localised to particular clients?

  - This approach has been used with a number of clients and examples are available via global knowledge management to 'IBMers'. However, it is not an official or packaged offering.

- How do you balance the managerial and operational requirements?

  - Delegates emphasised the need to balance the managerial and operational requirements and to obtain buy-in from clients when discussing and agreeing requirements/design. The CMS cuts across existing organisational units and silos in most organisations and this is something implementers will have to recognise and manage.

o One of the requirements is for 'stakeholder comfort', and unless you can deliver this for managerial and operations stakeholders you are unlikely to be successful. This requires incremental delivery of real value and effective communication with stakeholders throughout the project lifecycle.

- How do you manage the constant demands for status reports and reactive work required when something happens that takes funding and resources from being spent on the activities of defining and developing the CMS?

  o It is clear that there needs to be a maturity of process around implementing the CMS, not just a simple set of functional requirements and a piece of software that satisfies them. Any project has to deliver a solution that delivers a capability to manage change (new project) together with operational activities. The CM activity for status reporting helps to manage the demand for ad hoc reporting. Prioritisation of work should be based on operational and service level commitments. Projects that require status reports normally build the resource and cost of providing these into the project costs.

## CONCLUSION

This chapter documents a practical approach to defining the requirements for configuration management and a CMS. It suggests using a top-down approach, with use case workshops attended by key stakeholders, to define the process requirements and the required interactions with the CMS, in a structured way.

The top-down approach ensures that the business context and scope are identified. These help to ensure that the right stakeholders are involved in the implementation. This top-down approach also means that any governance issues around implementing the CMS are included and this helps to gain senior management buy-in and commitment (which is sometimes an issue with CMS implementations).

Identifying the CSFs and agreeing the basis for making strategic decisions during the life of the project helps to keep the focus on the real business needs and priorities. Managing the implementation as a project or programme of projects is important because the scope and assumptions are then defined at each stage. This helps to manage stakeholder expectations.

Salvage emphasised the need for a strong foundation for requirements gathering and the need for discovering the top-down vision for what the CMS should deliver. Defining the overall context and framework within which the CMS solution can be defined helps to keep the focus of requirements gathering on the real business needs. Without this, it is difficult to scope the work and engage the right stakeholders in the requirements gathering. With commitment from the right stakeholders, it is easier to build a business case and prioritise the work for each stage of implementation.

Configuration management provides information that will support other processes, so you will need to know what information these other processes require. As we can see from this session, a good way to do this is through a use case workshop for each process that the CMS needs to support. Use cases provide a structured approach to identifying the key interfaces, data requirements and roles associated with an activity. The use case approach helps to ensure that the requirements are defined at the right level, that is they should not be too technical, but they should still deliver a comprehensive and effective set of requirements.

Feedback from participants was very positive and there was great interest shown in the approach.

# 8   STRATEGY AND VISION

## OBJECTIVES

The objectives of this chapter are to get feedback on setting a vision and strategy for implementing configuration management and a CMS based on a case study from BT Global Services with BT Operate.

## SUMMARY

The vision for configuration management and the CMS is a key part of the overall service strategy for an organisation (see the ITIL Service Strategy volume, Chapter 4). The mapping of customer business outcomes to services and service assets can be accomplished as part of the CMS to support service management.

The case study demonstrated a top-down approach to clarifying and implementing a CM vision. It emphasised the idea that the roles and responsibilities of a configuration team should be defined up front as part of the CMS vision, rather than after tools have been deployed.

The delegates generally liked the approach taken in the case study but a view was expressed that perhaps the time has come for more radical innovation. In an ITIL-inspired organisation, focused on holistic business service delivery and business outcomes, a wider range of stakeholder needs have to be represented in the configuration team than used to be the case. Organisation, people and people skills should feature more in the strategic vision for the CMS.

## SERVICE ASSET AND CONFIGURATION MANAGEMENT VISIONS AND STRATEGIES

Mike Tomkinson (CM Beacon, BT Global Services) acknowledged the work from Jason Sutherland Rowe, a process consultant at BT Operate, who helped to develop the vision for how configuration management could be improved. BT Operate deploys and runs communications services for customers over BT's core network and systems.

Tomkinson pointed out to the delegates that the CMS 'vision' has to be a shared thing, but with a defined scope. The vision he presented related purely to configuration management and is not a pan-BT or customer-facing vision. However, it incorporated the views of other people in his organisation and in the industry. Nevertheless, an organisation can have only one directing vision: Tomkinson said, 'If you have two visions, you are either delusional or have double vision.'

A vision starts with a goal, in this case to 'provide robust management and control of IT assets information through cataloguing, auditing and recording change etc., and in doing so, provide accurate information to enable the efficient execution of ITIL processes to deliver services'.

To achieve this, the organisation wanted to ensure that standard methods, practices and processes (representing accepted 'good practice') are actually used, not just talked about. It also wanted to make sure that configuration information is kept up to date in an effective and timely way, without compromising the agility of other business processes, and that process improvement is institutionalised so as to maintain the organisation's ISO/IEC 20000, Sarbanes – Oxley (SOX) and ITIL compliance without compromising the competitiveness of the business.

The organisation hoped that other processes would be able to leverage timely and accurate information from the CMS in order to reduce cycle time and the risk of failure.

The issues the vision addressed were those around the current behaviours of the organisation that lead to poor planning and inadequate risk management. For example, people were not always using the 'best practice' processes, leading to poor quality configuration data and a CMS that was not trusted or used effectively.

Other current issues included focusing on inventories of data rather than on information about an end-to-end service and its users, that the scope of the CMS was too narrow (storing just technical hardware configuration, but neglecting software and applications), that configuration management was fragmented with multiple owners, and that there were no organisation-wide standards for naming and identification, leading to over-complicated reporting and poor communications. This resulted in labour-intensive activities, especially for the CM staff who had to spend time creating reports, verifying data and doing data uploads for users.

The net result of all this is that:

- the information in the CMS was unreliable;
- configuration management did not easily support other ITIL and general business processes across the organisation;
- service availability, quality and cycle times were unacceptable.

The new vision was implemented in terms of continual improvement (see the ITIL Continual Service Improvement volume for more guidance here).

The objectives were to reduce cycle times, to reduce the risk of failure and to deliver improvements for:

- the service desk (incident, problem, request management);
- service level management;
- asset management and finance (policies, usage, asset lifecycle, contracts, cost, budgeting);
- change and release management;
- capacity management (performance, utilisation).

The configuration process activities to be undertaken included:

- identification and definition of CIs, including service maps and legacy CIs;
- CMDB control (including categorisation of CMDB types, access controls and enforcement of process);
- CI status accounting, both at the macro level (on order, received, under repair, for disposal) and configuration level (past, current, future desired configuration state);
- verification of the CMS (spot audit checks of the CMDB against the operational infrastructure and design procedures, physical audits, validation of service maps and process etc.).

CI identification is the basis for a CMS vision and it is often a challenge. It is tempting to make everything you know about, or might want to know about, a CI, but this delivers a CMDB/CMS that is unwieldy and difficult to maintain. A recommended approach is to:

1 Design the configuration model for your CMS (an example is shown in Figure 8.1).

2 Identify the information that should be in it and will be used by the business and other CMS stakeholders to support your vision (not the information that could be in it).

3 Identify the business-critical products and services.

4 Identify your CIs top-down, service by service, so that you capture (and have to manage) the minimum information that will be useful (i.e. information that you are confident will be used). To start with, this will probably be just a few key CIs and related data (a subset of the possible CIs, just sufficient to deliver enough of your vision to be useful).

You now need a strategy for transforming the organisation from where it is now (all organisations have some sort of CMS, even if it is poorly defined, inconsistent across the organisation and rather dysfunctional) to where you want it to be, so you need to understand where you are now. You may be starting with a manual process and a stand-alone CM team heavily involved in administration, slow to support requests for change and with costly compliance audits necessary.

**Figure 8.1** Example of a configuration model

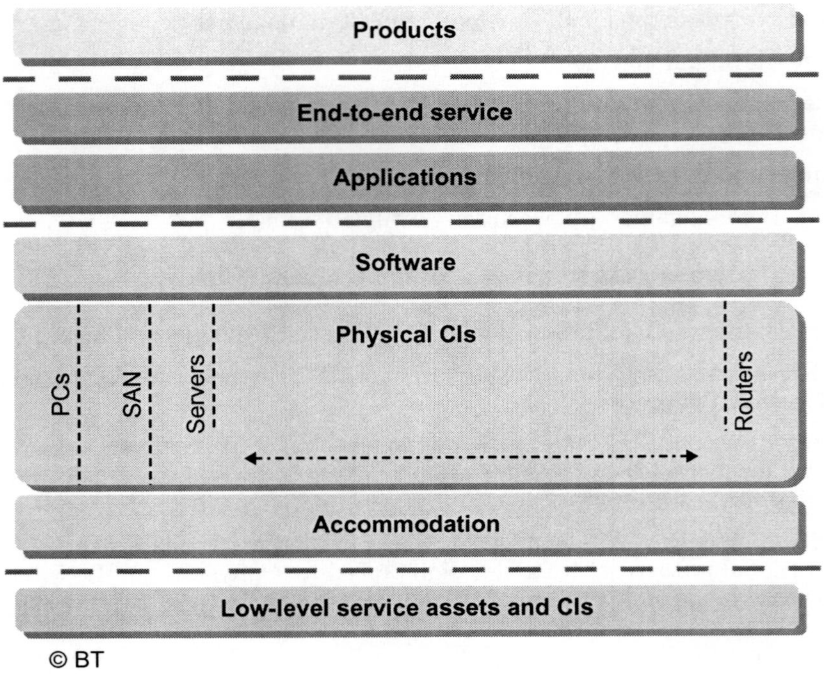

© BT

A staged transformation to where you want to be could be:

- Stage 1 delivers a 'fit for purpose' CM team, with semi-automated processes, good integration with project/portfolio management processes, more timely response to change and service requests (of the order of a week or less) and less need for a separate audit because the process delivers compliance information about itself.

- Stage 2 could deliver a 'best in class' CM team with full automation of key processes (e.g. discovery and reconciliation), integration with all relevant organisational processes, timely response to change and service requests (less than a day) and no requirement for separate audits.

- Stage 3 delivers a 'world class' CM team and adds full automation of proactive and autonomic (self-healing) processes, full integration with all relevant processes and organisation-wide, federated information repositories (e.g. a federated CMDB as envisaged in ITIL v3), near-real-time response to change and service requests, and fully supported and reusable tools.

Achieving the desired future state is really about delivering process automation. You should be able to document your high-level vision and future states on a single page. You can then use this to validate lower level implementation decisions (do they help to make your vision come true?). An example of future states with process automation is shown in Table 8.1.

**Table 8.1** Example of future states with process automation

| Process support | Process capability | Type of automation |
| --- | --- | --- |
| Change management and configuration management (to implement release and change management) | Requests for Change supported by risk and impact assessment with a record of the desired future state (after the change/release). | Semi-automated.<br><br>Diagrammatic representation of assets and configurations.<br><br>Ability to select CIs from the CMDB (validates entry).<br><br>Ability to determine impact and identify approval groups (for CIs. changes, releases).<br><br>Ability to calculate and flag risk. |
| Change management and configuration management (synchronise the CMDB with the live services and environment) | Compare end-state to expected state/baseline to check they are the same.<br><br>Commit configuration changes to the CMDB and Definitive Media Library (DML).<br><br>If there is a difference: intervene, review, reconcile and take action (e.g. commit/rollback). | Automated:<br><br>Reconciliation engine;<br><br>Update CMDB – CIs, dynamic maps, statuses etc.<br><br>Semi-automated:<br><br>Manually manage a small percentage of exceptions. |
| Enables incident management, problem management, service level management | Up-to-date information available to other processes.<br><br>Maintenance of data outside the formal IT change process (e.g. business-related information – still controlled and audited). | Semi-automated.<br><br>Other processes integrate with the configuration management process and the CMDB to automatically and automatically use the information.<br><br>Updates made to the CMDB by processes (e.g. monitoring, Service Level Management, capacity management). |

Your vision should consider the key roles involved:

- **The CM team.** The CM team will carry out spot checks or audits to verify that processes are being adhered to. It will own and maintain diagrammatic service maps showing the end-to-end operation of key services and the organisation's future plans for them. It will own and enforce naming conventions. It will ensure that the process and CMS adequately supports other core processes, where applicable, with timely, reliable and accurate information. It will oversee and, possibly, provide awareness sessions and training for configuration management, its benefits and its associated 'good practices'.

- **Configuration managers.** Configuration managers own the configuration data for a platform or end-to-end service. They are responsible for the accuracy of the data and they reconcile any issues or anomalies in the data.

- **Change implementers.** Change implementers are responsible for ensuring that change tickets are completed accurately for any change or release. They are also responsible for ensuring that the data in the CMS is updated in a timely manner after any change or release and they are responsible for correcting any errors or anomalies in the CMS data, if possible; if not, for bringing them to the attention of the configuration manager or the CM team.

There are several key enablers for the realisation of your vision that should be in place. First and foremost, buy-in and sponsorship from senior management is vital, not just for the CMS but for the necessary cultural change from configuration management as a bureaucratic process to configuration management as an enabler for business change. You should be able to form a reasoned view of the maturity of your process and CMS, as a basis against which to assess future improvements.

Then you must have sufficient controls in place to manage your assets from acquisition to retirement, and critical services must be defined (with service maps). This probably includes having a documented strategy for the federation or replacement of existing repositories.

You should define key roles (such as configuration manager) ahead of tool acquisition. As Tomkinson says, 'Fit the tool to the task, not the task to the tool.' CI ownership must be clarified, agreed and communicated, naming conventions and governance processes established and the CMS and asset management brought under a single owner, if possible.

The key benefits from your CMS vision should be the delivery of a 'single view of the truth' (as opposed to the existence of pockets of data of varying quality), support for other ITIL processes, better compliance and more effective security through more effective recording and tracking of assets, better availability from better (more informed) risk management, more accurate information to support better benefit–cost management, lower costs through more effective utilisation of assets and removal of unused assets.

Useful KPIs might be the reduction of the number and severity of incidents, the reduction in high impact incidents, lower costs through better utilisation of IT assets, and less money spent on costly audits.

After Tomkinson's presentation, the delegates were asked to discuss their own visions for the CMS.

## CONTRIBUTORS TO THE INTERACTIVE SESSION

Eleven contributors to the discussion represented the practitioner community. They included representatives from Unilever, NWDC, DeltaRail Group Limited, BT, Serco NTCC, Renault UK, EADS DS UK Ltd, HMPS, Principia IT and Fidelity Investments.

## PARTICIPATING PRACTITIONER COMMUNITY FEEDBACK

The delegates' thoughts about the positive aspects of the presentation identified:

- a clear positive approach: obviously tying into a good ITIL v3 and maturity model structure;
- a presentation grounded in reality: 'warts and all';
- that the roles and responsibilities of the CM team should be defined up front, rather than after a tool has been deployed;
- that it showed from real life that you have to have a dedicated team looking after configuration management, and that it's not something that can be done by a few people in their slack time;
- that some common difficulties and thoughts were highlighted;
- that other companies are experiencing similar difficulties to those the delegates were experiencing.

The delegates liked the idea that the roles and responsibilities of the CM team should be defined up front, as part of the vision, rather than after tools have been deployed. Quite apart from anything else, this promotes a focus on 'business outcomes' rather than the needs of any particular tool (or a particular vendor's marketing group).

Delegates also thought that the case study showed, from real life, that often you have to have a dedicated team looking after configuration management. However, this begged the question 'What about smaller organisations?'. One answer might be that smaller organisations don't need CMS, because with only a few people, configuration can manage itself.

We think, nevertheless, that a vision is still important, even in the smallest organisations, but if the organisation is small enough, it may be a part-time responsibility for a manager, supported by the facilities built into appropriate tools. The vision is still important, even for a smaller company, because a separate

CM team can then evolve as the company grows. If this can happen without compromising a stated vision, disruption of the CMS during growth is less likely.

One interesting issue was whether the vision behind the case study is too conventional. 'You talked of culture change,' one delegate said, 'but the CM team roles remained the same. The new challenges require new roles driven by the skill sets needed to create, maintain and understand end-to-end [change]. The configuration team would begin to include operations and technical support skills as well as business process and business application knowledge.' The point being made was that in an ITIL-inspired organisation, focused on holistic business service delivery and business outcomes, a wider range of stakeholder needs have to be represented in the CM team and that people and people skills need to feature more in the strategic vision.

Insights from the delegates included:

- People/cultural changes are tied to changes in CMS functionality and tooling. It is important to see how the skill sets, competences and behaviours of the organisation's staff map onto the formal configuration management roles, and how they mature and change as the CMS is institutionalised.

- It's necessary to formally identify configuration managers in the organisation. They are different people to the overall configuration manager/process owner. One delegate's experience of doing this successfully for incident and problem management suggested that this really moves configuration management to a new level quite quickly.

- There is a question as to whether it is worthwhile implementing a CMDB for an environment where all hardware and network elements are contractually supported by third parties and the change is restricted to applications/ functionality etc.

  o We think the CMDB can still usefully hold information about CIs for elements that are contractually supported by third parties because this supports change, release, problem and service level management of assets that both organisations are concerned about. However, you would only worry about defining CIs to a level of detail (granularity) useful to you, for your CMDB (although, perhaps in more mature organisations, you could federate to your third party's CMDBs, if this provided benefits to your business).

- A concern was whether automation reduces buy-in to the process and makes you rely too heavily on the tools. One delegate wondered if people would say, 'I don't need to update the CMDB because the auto-discovery tool will find it!'

  o We think that this is a possible issue, but it should be addressed by proper management of the vision and stakeholder buy-in, and by making awareness sessions and training in configuration management available. There is also a risk that automated activities are not updated in a timely manner, and people implement manual workarounds that become complex and bureaucratic.

Tomkinson then challenged the delegates by asking two questions:

- 'If you had to create a vision for a CMS, what would be your starting point?';
- 'What would be the key activities needed to create and implement your vision?'

At least one delegate suggested that where Tomkinson was now would be a good starting place, reflecting the possibility that building a CMS vision from scratch, in a greenfield environment, will not always be easy. Nevertheless, delegates managed to suggest several possible starting points for the formulation of a useful vision:

- The organisation's customers' needs and the needs of the business (what the customer wants us to deliver and in what time frame).
- Building a service catalogue around existing individual CMDBs for different sets of 'nuts and bolts', and then joining the catalogue and the CMDBs (this may be a little technology focused as a starting point).
- An explanation of why other business/technology processes will be flawed and not deliver full benefits without a CMS.
- An understanding of what it is we are trying to achieve and of definite target dates for delivering palpable improvement (smart milestones, for example 'In 2014, we will…').
- Recognition of the limitations of the status quo (such as a potential for rapid growth and volume/scale increases that cannot be managed in the existing situation).
- A project plan and defined drivers for improvement (don't let the capabilities of a particular tool drive the process).
- Studying 'best practice' was suggested as a key activity for the creation and implementation of the vision.

    o We suggest that the ITIL volumes are a good place to find this. Remember the idea of 'fit for purpose'. If what you have is 'good practice', this may be sufficient for your needs.

Understanding what you are trying to do and the options available to you are very important. Before starting to create and implement a vision, you must ensure that the current and future needs of the organisation are understood and establish where your present systems don't deliver (and perhaps benchmark your environment against competitors). You should identify existing processes and attempt to reuse, or build on, them. One delegate suggested that you should 'measure and persecute [configuration] data owners', which is perhaps a bit extreme but does recognise the fact that the owners of configuration data are responsible for maintaining their information or others may view the CMS with distrust. They must be brought onside and convinced that the vision is of real benefit to them and the organisation (don't overlook the importance of charismatic people and persuasion skills to the implementation of your vision).

Specific suggestions from the delegates included:

- Restrict the scope initially and allow it to grow slowly to meet the full required scope over time.
- Try to implement consolidated data and a clear process.
- Make sure that you only consider and hold what is clearly needed in order to deliver defined benefit.
- Ensure that the vision is translated into SMART objectives (i.e. objectives that are: Specific, Measurable, Agreed, Realistic and Time-specific).
- Highlight process conformance issues that impact the CMS.
- A feasibility study and proof of concept will help market and demonstrate the vision and goals (or, at least, set some scope), but beware of the attitude that tools are the entire solution.
- Identify configuration managers and build from the service down, closing the gap between services and (local) CMDBs. Consider also costs management and licence management as issues driving CMS acceptance.

Finally, delegates pointed out that money drives most things in business today (even people issues have monetary implications), so put a monetary value on anything you want to achieve.

## CONCLUSION

This case study provided a useful insight into setting a vision for configuration management for a large global organisation. It demonstrates a top-down approach to clarifying and implementing improvements in stages to deliver business outcomes such as reduced cycle times and reduced risk of failure.

The vision for configuration management is comprehensive and recognises that robust management and control of IT asset and configurations will provide accurate information to enable the efficient execution of other processes, in this case ITIL, to deliver services. This vision is a key part of the overall service strategy for an organisation. Mapping customer business outcomes to services and service assets as part of the CMS implementation enables people to visualise and understand the end-to-end service, how it is made up, as well as the risks and impact of changes, problems and incidents.

Many CM implementations need to place more emphasis on the organisation and culture shift required to deliver a CMS. By defining the organisation, roles and responsibilities up front, the right capabilities and resources can be designed and built into the solution, rather than after CMS tools have been deployed.

The delegates generally liked the approach taken in the case study, but a view was expressed that perhaps the time has come for more radical innovation. In an ITIL-inspired organisation, focused on holistic business service delivery and business outcomes, a wider range of stakeholder needs have to be represented in the CM team than used to be the case. Organisation and people capabilities should now feature more in the strategic vision for the CMS.

The staged approach to implementing improvements works well in practice. The scope of the initial stages can be contained to supporting change and release management with processes that are semi-automated. The next stage is to automate more of the activities that will free up people and resources to use on the third stage of implementation: support for incident, problem and service level management.

# 9 SELECTING CMS TOOLS

## OBJECTIVE

The objective of this chapter is to describe a process for the selection of tools for a Configuration Management System (CMS) that will satisfy the needs of its business and technical stakeholders.

## SUMMARY

This chapter describes a fairly conventional market appraisal, tool appraisal and pilot study process. However, the key to success is defining the scope properly and engaging all the relevant people. The focus of the selection process is on setting expectations through prior planning, on information gathering as a prerequisite for making a choice, and on balancing objective and subjective decision-making.

A key requirement for success is that the selection process is properly budgeted and resourced. It is not something that should be done informally, in someone's 'spare time'. Selecting the right application or tool satisfies all stakeholders.

## A BASIC IMPLEMENTATION PROCESS

An initial overview presentation on this topic by John Metcalfe (Mentor IT Ltd and CMSG Committee Member) was made to the delegates. Its main focuses were:

- on setting expectations through prior planning;
- on information gathering as a prerequisite for making a choice;
- on balancing objective and subjective decision-making.

Chapters 7 and 11 also support the selection of CMS tools.

According to Metcalfe, the first thing that project management needs to do is to define the scope (in both organisational and process terms) of the tools selection process and get budget approval for the entire scope. You should assume that anything that is not budgeted for simply will not happen. As well as choosing a tool you need to:

- budget and plan how to demonstrate due diligence in the selection process;
- develop the business case for the CMS tool in discussion with business stakeholders in the CMS;
- obtain business sponsorship;
- fund the selection process;
- involve the different departments that could be impacted by your choice.

You will need a range of expertise available to you:

- Technical and subject matter experts;
- Project managers;
- Analysts;
- Designers;
- Specification writers;
- Testers etc.

Technology managers sometimes want to look firstly at tools from the major incumbent tool supplier, then at the last vendor that visited and, finally, at something from the top of a Google® search page. If you merely have the resources necessary to make a choice between such a list of 'obvious' commercial tools, you may find that no one is happy with your choice at the end of the selection process. It is also possible that you may have chosen the wrong tool with the wrong scope for what the organisation requires, not only now but in a few years' time.

To a large extent, success in CMS tool selection is all about managing expectations and scope: services, customers, functions, technology platforms, locations, processes. There are many sources of expectations to manage:

- The people in your company have expectations: your operations and support people, developers, your Change, Configuration and Release Management (CCRM) community, your business users, your legal department.
- Your partners have expectations: suppliers, customers, software vendors, outsourcing providers.
- Process support: for example change, configuration, release and deployment management, other service management processes, development process.
- Products come with CMS expectations: consider managed applications, different media, infrastructure, documentation requirements.
- Sites and locations that will be affected (although in a mature organisation everywhere would be within the scope of the CMS).

There are expectations for the knowledge and information that will be delivered from the CMS and tool choice:

- Why does someone want information?
- When do they want it?
- How do they want the information delivered and how do they want to access it?
- Where is the information required?
- Who wants the information?
- Which information do they want?

After the selection process, there must be no doubt as to why the CMS was chosen and what it is expected to do.

The essential reason for having a CMS is that it lets you answer questions about the configuration and integrity of the technology that runs your business. Unless you know what you are running where, how it is configured, when and why it was changed and who by, you are unable to claim any sort of real governance of your business systems. Your CMS tools must support your organisation's governance and your selection process must determine how well the competing tools succeed in this. They should support risk management and should help to mitigate or manage any risk resulting from an inappropriate or out-of-date configuration reaching production.

The CMS tools need to support the delivery of palpable benefits in terms of quantified financial benefits, performance benefits and more clearly defined service level targets. Your evaluation should consider the total lifecycle cost of ownership (including evaluation cost, maintenance and upgrade) for the various tools under consideration, together with their organisational and cultural impacts.

Once you know the expectations of the various stakeholders in the CMS solution, you can start to gather the requirements for a tool and other information necessary to balance subjectivity with objectivity during the selection process. Techniques that you use to clarify the requirements for the CMS itself (such as use case workshops, see Chapter 7) can also be used to help clarify the requirements for a CMS tool. The techniques you will use for gathering this information will differ for different stakeholders:

- Business sponsors can be interviewed (using someone that fits into the business culture and who can discuss CMS issues in business terms). Their requirements can also be gathered from analysis of project planning deliverables and from use case workshops.
- For the IT organisation, you can interview key stakeholders (again, using someone who understands the culture), analyse project review documentation and hold use case workshops to explore particular scenarios.

- For service management, you can review or instigate process audits, review service issues and set up use case workshops.

You can then investigate the characteristics of key applications using research and industry reports, establish the infrastructure the CMS tool must operate within (using infrastructure audits, by reading the current CI list and by talking to technical architects), and you can establish the requirements for hardware, software and document management using process audits, reviews and use case workshops.

Delegate feedback on common requirements for the CMS, including those in the initial presentation, is reported below. This forms part of the requirements gathering process.

The process for getting to a good decision once you know what expectations people have for a CMS tool (that is once you have done the groundwork thoroughly) is comparatively simple. You should budget and plan for a three-stage approach (market appraisal, tool appraisal, pilot installation), stick to the plan, and lock down communications (to avoid the organisation becoming swamped with vendors lobbying their solution at various perceived decision makers in the organisation).

### Stage 1 Market appraisal
Information for this stage can be gathered from websites (try visiting the BCS/CMSG website, CM Crossroads or, of course, Google® and vendors' websites), but you can also use independent industry (analyst) reports, such as those from Gartner and Bloor, or visit exhibitions. Be very aware of the inherent (and sometimes less than obvious) bias in these sources. Google®, for example, is probably biased towards information designed to be found by marketing departments clued-up on how search engines work.

The appraisal itself should be based on a top-level checklist, which is essentially:

- a functionality filter for five or six key capabilities (e.g. change management, problem management, release management, build management, deployment management, version control, baselines etc.);
- a check for a solution structure (e.g. single/multiple products, database solution) that fits within your overall CMS architecture;
- a check against corporate constraints (such as preferred vendors);
- the results of an initial demonstration with key stakeholders.

You should aim to end up with a shortlist containing about four possible tools/vendors.

### Stage 2 Tool appraisal
Appraisal proper should start by distributing a Request for Information (RFI) to the tool vendors on your shortlist. The RFI should request a simple 'Yes/No/At

a Cost' type response to requirement statements, and provide typical use cases, which will become a basis for future demonstrations. You can also explore known product weaknesses and should try to get access to independent reference sites. Even if a reference site is chosen by the vendors ('techies don't lie to techies'), if you approach a reference site with someone technically competent, its 'techies' will proudly talk about the workarounds needed to get their CMS operational. This highlights any weak points of the products involved.

There is a risk of drowning in information, so information gathering must be managed by a skilled, experienced practitioner who can prioritise what is important. Analysis can use a 'must/should/could' approach (see 'MoSCoW Method' in Resources) with a weighted scoring scheme for 'shoulds' and 'coulds'. 'Pairwise comparison' (see 'Pairwise comparison' in Resources) can be another effective way to prioritise requirements without the intrusion of politics. It is a good idea to use a tool to support this as pairwise comparisons can be clumsy if done by hand. The aim is to get the selection down to the 'best of two'.

You should ask for a demonstration of your final vendors' proposed solutions and check against the RFI criteria and specified use cases. This will confirm that your selection criteria have been met and give you confidence to progress to Stage 3.

### Stage 3 Pilot installations
Final selection should be based on pilot studies. You would expect to pilot only one solution, but if the first pilot fails then it is recommended that you have a risk budget and plan for a second pilot.

Specify the installation and initial configuration for these pilots. Be careful to avoid biasing one pilot environment to a particular choice. For example if the highest scoring choice is very memory intensive and the runner-up critically dependent on disk performance, trading off memory for faster disks in the infrastructure pilot could ensure that the second choice wins out.

Start with the top scorer, monitor the installation, test it with established use cases, and obtain user feedback on its attributes. If the first pilot fails to satisfy the requirements, then pilot the second product.

Then review and close the selection process and make sure that the results are clearly communicated to all the stakeholders, together with documented authority from appropriate management.

### Key selection issues
Things to watch out for during the selection of CMS tools and in the final review are presented in Table 9.1.

**Table 9.1** Key selection issues

| Managing expectations | Requirement and information gathering |
| --- | --- |
| Know who the real decision makers are (these may not be you). | Prevent scope creep. |
| You will need sponsors/crusaders at all levels. | Understand the full impact of the CMS on the business. |
| Know your own internal buying process and the key players in it. | Avoid over-long specifications. |
| Ensure that the Annual Operating Plan includes your project. | Stick to **what** you want to do, not **how** the tool should do it. |
| | Focus on how the tool will be used to deliver the benefits. |

| Market appraisal | Pilot installations |
| --- | --- |
| Define your terms using industry standard terms (see ISO standards, ITIL). | Do not assume that the vendor knows and understands your processes. |
| Remember that sales volumes and market position may not show the whole truth. | Do not outsource partner involvement – it will not be free. |
| Beware of trying to know everything about the product – be selective. | |
| Beware of making one product a winner too early. | |
| Assess the company and its supporting services as well as its products/tools. | |

**Resources**

Resources on standard product evaluation can be found at:

- Commercial Off-The-Shelf (COTS) software evaluation: *A process for COTS software product evaluation* by Santiago Comella-Dorda, John Dean, Grace Lewis, Edwin Morris, Patricia Oberndorf, Erin Harper, July 2004. www.sei.cmu.edu/pub/documents/03.reports/pdf/03tr017.pdf

- MoSCoW Method, http://en.wikipedia.org/wiki/MoSCoW_Method
- Pairwise comparison, http://en.wikipedia.org/wiki/Pairwise_comparison

More information can be found at:

- CM Crossroads Change and Configuration Management Tools WIKI: www.cmcrossroads.com/cgi-bin/cmwiki/view/CM/CmTools
- CM Crossroads Wiki-Web: www.cmcrossroads.com/cgi-bin/cmwiki/view/CM/
- CM Crossroads Forum: www.cmcrossroads.com/component/option,com_fireboard/Itemid,593/func,showcat/catid,506/

## CONTRIBUTORS TO THE INTERACTIVE SESSION

Eleven contributors to the discussion represented the practitioner community. They included representatives from Axios Systems, NWDC, BAE, Capgemini, Principia IT, HMPS, Plymouth City Council, DeltaRail Group Limited and ESM.

## PARTICIPATING PRACTITIONER COMMUNITY FEEDBACK

Delegates were invited to give feedback on the presentation.

### This is what I liked about what I heard

- 'Liked the three-stage approach.'
- 'Confirmation I am on the right path.'
- 'The presentation set out a clear and usable process for selecting and getting a CMS tool.'
- 'Use of Use Cases.'
- 'Liked stepwise approach.'
- 'Demonstrated a clear and logical approach.'
- 'Pleasing to see that some of the actions we have recently taken are mirrored in the presentation. Adds (a little) confidence that we're heading the right way.'
- 'Good presentation.'
- 'The presentation has covered much of the ground that we're covering now, which is a good indication that we're going in the right direction, but also gives some hints about where we're going and what to do about some of the problems we're likely to encounter.'

The process documented in this chapter was presented to conference attendees for computer-assisted discussion. From this, the experience of CM community participants in this area can be captured (readers can 'cherry pick' requirements and issues relevant to their particular circumstances) and the basic processes validated.

## What is the scope of the tools selection process?

This was discussed in terms of:

- organisation;

- process;

- organisational scope.

In organisational terms, the delegates accepted that providing information for the various stakeholders is of prime importance and that any tool should be easy to use (without compromising delivery of the CMS). Specific areas that the tool evaluation must deal with were identified as:

- support for roles and functions;

- development teams;

- business users;

- service management;

- operations and support;

- service desk (or help desk);

- build and release managers;

- change and configuration management team;

- facilitating project control;

- support for impact assessments;

- support for the CM team, integration with existing CM databases, ideally with automated discovery and reconciliation with any existing or evolving CMDB product or system;

- integration with change and incident management (the ability to assign defects to revisions, to identify problematic revisions for the help/service desk);

- role-based (as opposed to person-based) access controls.

The delegates agreed on the necessity for finding the compelling business reasons behind acquiring any CMS tools. 'How can you identify the scope of tools until you have defined the overall goal?' was one comment. Delegates agreed with the necessity for stakeholder buy-in (which involves identifying a chief stakeholder or sponsor in the business).

## Common requirements for selecting CMS tools

The delegates then brainstormed 'common requirements for CMS tools'. This provided a starting point for selecting 'requirements' for the specific tools selection process. It is not a 'tool selection checklist', merely a pragmatic selection of features that practitioners in the field thought might prove useful.

## Business benefit

- **Business benefit.** A successful tool will provide visible benefit with its introduction and use. It should display benefit, in business terms, to the business stakeholders and support the documented business need.

- **Cost-effectiveness.** A CMS tool should provide a foundation for creating and controlling service management and delivery standards and policies throughout the organisation. The implementation should increase confidence in the reliability of the information and data held. The delegates emphasised that a tool should be as cost-effective as possible, as far as is consistent with operational effectiveness.

## General support for the business and service management

- **Baselining.** A tool should also facilitate the baselining of service(s), environment(s), processes and provide reports and documentation to support incremental improvement and change. Without an 'as is' baseline to compare against it is difficult to show a return on investment or manage process improvement.

- **Governance.** CMS tools should support good governance. They should:

  o be auditable and support strong portfolio management, asset management, change management and version control;

  o provide an authoritative source of data to incident and problem management processes, and service level management;

  o be monitoring tools;

  o document the change history of CIs.

- **Lifecycle support.** A CMS needs to deal with the holistic lifecycle, not just part of it. A tool should:

  o be able to maintain multiple states for a CI-based on its lifecycle;

  o provide workflows that maintain CI lifecycle integration with change management.

- **Single source.** The CMS should provide an authoritative source of information, 'one version of the truth', that underpins IT service management.

- **Service structure.** A services focus is an emerging business trend. A tool needs the ability to maintain and support the service structure used by the business.

## CMS architecture and design requirements

- **Abstraction.** In order to reduce complexity and encourage reuse across organisational silos, a CMS tool should:

- o provide an information model and keep metadata on CIs with the supporting processes;
- o have an open Application Programming Interface (API) that can be accessed externally;
- o have a consistent internal structural model itself.

- **Adapability.** The delegates recognised the importance of adaptability to meet changing business and technology needs. For example, the CMS should provide adequate reporting functions to enable the solution to adapt to changing needs.

- **Architecture.** The CMS tools should fit within the overall architecture of the organisation's CMS. ITIL provides an example of a CMS architecture with a presentation layer, knowledge processing layer, information integration layer and facilities to integrate federated sources of information and data (see Figure 2.1). If a tool overlaps with another tool significantly, then see what can be done to contain the scope (e.g. make some modules inaccessible).

- **Distribution.** Many organisations are changing towards a web-based, distributed culture, so a CMS tool should support distributed teams and web-based access across different locations, and provide a capability for displaying multiple locations, devices or connections per user.

- **Flexibility.** Your requirements will change. Look for flexibility in workflow definition and report generation to support different processes (e.g. agile; ITIL) and to support updatable workflows.

- **Integration.** Any CMS tool should integrate cleanly with other tools because silos of data are inefficient. Consider 'out of the box' integrations (e.g. with Integrated Development Environments – IDEs), with discovery tools, interfaces to lifecycle QA/testing tools, provision of a reconciliation engine to federate data from multiple sources. 'Can I integrate several data sources, reporting tools etc. through the same presentation facility?' Consider the integration method to be used with suppliers to minimise duplication.

- **Integrity.** Any information or tool repository must offer database-style information and data integrity, possibly across multiple data sources, and support the creation of one version of the truth that underpins the IT services and products to be delivered.

- **Relationships.** The maintenance of associations between CIs and associated records (such as known errors and changes) is of fundamental importance to the CMS.

- **Resilience.** The tool should be reliable ('it mustn't crash or lose data'), be robust in the event of systems failure or external disaster, provide a strong 'disaster recovery' story, and support effective administrative functionality for backup/restore and failover etc.

- **Scalability.** A tool should not suffer from inherent barriers to scalability either in technology terms (data volumes, performance) or in user terms (for large, possibly distributed, teams).

- **Security.** The information in the CMS is business critical and the organisation's standards for information security should apply. A tool should provide:

  o role-based access to CIs;

  o role-based access to the tool and integration with company security (directory services etc.) generally;

  o maintenance of the rights of users to changes to data;

  o restriction of 'who can do what' to a subset of the full functionality that is applicable to a particular user;

  o a good security model that is flexible enough to accommodate different kinds of user (typically operations, developers, management, audit).

## Process scope

- **Process.** The tools should support core processes, yet be able to expand as business requirements evolve. The processes addressed by CMS tools should be aligned to recognisable/stated business goals (this is an important prerequisite for successful tool selection). The toolset may include full support for a process or integrate with an existing capability. Support for the following processes should be considered in addition to other lifecycle processes such as design, development and testing:

  o asset management;

  o change management;

  o configuration management;

  o decision support;

  o defect tracking;

  o financial governance and financial asset management;

  o incident management;

  o management information (business strategy);

  o problem management;

  o procurement;

  o release and deployment management;

  o risk management;

  o service level management integrated with availability management;

  o service measurement and reporting.

## User requirements

- **Accessibility.** In order to facilitate wide and appropriate use, a tool must be accessible to its users. This includes support for disabled employees.

- **Presentation.** An effective presentation layer is important for 'institutionalising' the use of tools. The tool should provide:

  o appropriate, and distinct, views to different stakeholders with different functional needs;

  o a graphical user interface (GUI);

  o a graphical service-level view;

  o a change impact view.

- **Reporting.** Good reporting facilities are essential to institutionalising a CMS tool. It should provide a user-friendly and powerful GUI, and verification of data and feedback of discrepancies via discovery tool.

- **Usability.** Ease of use. In order for a tool to be effective, it must allow intended users to accomplish their tasks in the best way possible. This depends on a number of factors including how well the functionality fits user needs, how well the flow through the application fits user tasks, and how well the response of the application fits user expectations.

- **Views.** Present the appropriate view to the appropriate user.

### Implementation/people requirements

- **Administration.** Low overhead administration should be a feature of any tool. Some tools require significant resources to administer complex environments.

- **Customisation.** It should be easy to update workflows.

- **Installation.** A tool should be reasonably easy to install and configure. Although the initial installation will be done in only a few environments, the time and process to upgrade an installation can be business critical. It is often a good idea to ask reference sites about upgrades.

- **Non-invasive.** Any tools should have minimal impact on operational systems. Tools should collect metrics unobtrusively with minimal impact on business service levels. In particular, they should not impact on the performance of production systems.

- **Supplier support.** The availability of good vendor or open-source community support is important. Will the vendor put your enhancements into their standard product and is there a roadmap for future development?

- **Training.** Training is a better way of spreading 'good practice' than any number of written directives, so effective training should be available for any tool.

## CONCLUSION

The three-stage approach to selecting a CMS was recommended by the delegates. This endorsed the clear and usable process for obtaining CMS tools presented in this chapter, based on, in particular:

- the exploration of 'use cases';
- adoption of a stepwise approach to tool selection.

It is also clear that many people involved in tool selection, even those with experience in the process, need to be 'comfortable' and confident that they are following the right path. Selecting CMS tools can be seen as risky (the CMS is very visible to the business and choices can impact the efficiency and effectiveness with which business and service automation is delivered). One real concern identified by the delegates was that tool selection is often heavily influenced by the culture and politics of the organisation. Often the CMS tools are marketed with a very technical focus, without clear links to business value, and this can hinder selection of a CMS as well as management commitment and sponsorship.

However, the point was also made that CMS tool selection is very much a standard product evaluation process to deliver a solution; why should it be different to selecting any other automated process tool or application? There are several reasons for this difference.

- CMS tools need to support the underlying IT (applications, database, infrastructure) and enable automation of the technical element with the process activities. This typically affects the tools that directly access or control the IT elements (e.g. software version control, release and deployment tools, discovery and audit tools).
- Many stakeholders in the CMS have technical backgrounds and tend to focus on the more technical aspects, because that is where they feel comfortable.
- A CMS cuts across business and technical silos. Perhaps there is often a need for 'positive discrimination' in favour of the business-oriented aspects of the choice.

One issue the delegates identified is the power of the status quo. 'Big organisations deliver successfully every day. How do you convince them they need a centralised tool for stuff they manage in their silos?' was one comment. It is easy to select tools that simply support the technical status quo, but which may form an actual barrier to the implementation of a holistic CMS or CM process. The lesson here is not to begin the tool selection process until the organisation is mature enough to recognise that it needs a CMS to support an integrated solution and some basic processes have been implemented across the organisation (i.e. the initial battles over process have been won). When an organisation reaches a certain level of service management capability inefficiencies that are caused by operating in silos become more visible. Buying a tool because it features well in the press or has a well-known company behind it, and then hoping that a CMS will sprout automatically and grow to fit it may be a mistake.

Quantifying the objectives and requirements for an overall solution and tool selection can help concentrate everyone's mind, but do not neglect the politics involved. Selecting or rejecting particular tools can add to or take away from particular managers' empires, and this must be managed sensitively if you are to succeed. Some vendors are more politically aware than others, which may help you with your tools acquisition process (as long as the vendor isn't manipulating company politics to its own agenda, with senior management, behind your back).

Governance of IT, as part of corporate governance, is going to be of increasing importance. The CMS is at the very heart of this. People and processes come before tools, but automation and tool support is an important part of institutionalising the CMS. This makes appropriate and defensible tool selection a key success factor for effective change and configuration management in practice.

# 10 POPULATING A CMDB: PROCESS DESIGN

## OBJECTIVES

The objectives of this chapter are to identify and debate issues relating to populating a CMDB and designing a process to support maintenance of the information in the CMS.

## SUMMARY

This chapter deals with identifying the definitive data for a CMS and with identifying the data and process gaps between where you are now and where you want to be. It then looks at some of the practical issues associated with process design and populating a CMDB, using the experience of the assembled delegates. It reports the delegates' experience of the weak points in their processes for maintaining configuration information and explores the key inhibitors you may meet in the real world and gives some mitigation strategies to deal with them.

## HOW DO YOU POPULATE YOUR CMDB?

Harvey Davison (of Lloyds TSB) conducted a brainstorming session on the process for populating a CMDB with the data/information needed for a CMS. The session was built around a sample CMDB structure, data source framework and process framework. The aim was to identify ways of improving a current process framework using gap analysis techniques and to explore ways of improving process maturity.

He presented an example of process engineering for delegates to brainstorm around two specific questions: 'What are my key inhibitors?' and 'What will I do differently tomorrow?'. The latter leading to the formulation of an action plan.

A sample CMDB structure (Figure 10.1) was used to illustrate the presentation.

**Figure 10.1** Sample CMDB structure

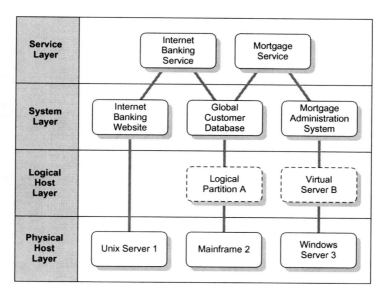

Examples for each layer shown in Figure 10.1 are:

- **Service layer.** Internet banking service/Mortgage service.
- **System layer.** Internet banking website/Global customer database/Mortgage administration system.
- **Logical host layer.** [not applicable]/Logical partition A/Virtual server B.
- **Physical host layer.** Unix server 1/Mainframe 2/Windows server 3.

Davison suggested that you first think about identifying your definitive data for each configuration item. For each CI type, this should include the detailed data/information and status as well as the relationships between the items. An example is shown in Figure 10.2.

Examples of the items details are:

- **Service layer.** There will be SLAs for the Internet banking service.
- **System layer.** Design information for the global customer database that the Internet banking service uses.
- **Logical host layer.** The automated inventory scanning database provides entries for the logical partition it resides in.
- **Physical host layer.** The data centre inventory provides entries for the mainframe, perhaps, which hosts this logical partition.

**Figure 10.2** Identifying definitive data diagram

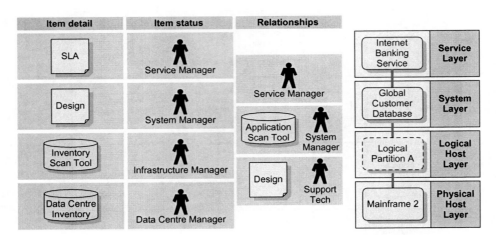

The item status in each layer is the responsibility of the service, systems, infrastructure and data centre manager, respectively.

The key data in the CMDB, which makes it different to a simple flat file of configuration data, relates to the relationships around configurations. Thus:

- the service manager relates the service and the SLAs to the design;
- the system manager, with the help of an application scan tool, relates the design to the infrastructure;
- the support technician, with the help of the design documentation, relates the service design to the logical and physical infrastructure.

You then need to define your process framework, which should describe your route from where you are now to the achievement of your vision. You can use your model of your definitive data as the basis for a gap analysis of the process, data and/or information, looking for the areas most in need of process improvement, using the colours red, green and amber: red (needs serious attention); amber (good enough for the time being); green (OK). Each box for item detail, item status and relationships on a diagram like Figure 10.2 would be marked red, amber or green. This provides a good visual display of any gaps as shown in Figure 10.3.

Davison asked the delegates to think about the gaps or weaknesses in the maturity of their own process and data/information, identifying the data type affected (service, system, logical or hardware/physical). He suggested categorising the gaps by whether they affected item detail, item status or relationships, and prioritising them as high, medium or low.

**Figure 10.3** Gap analysis using red/amber/green identification

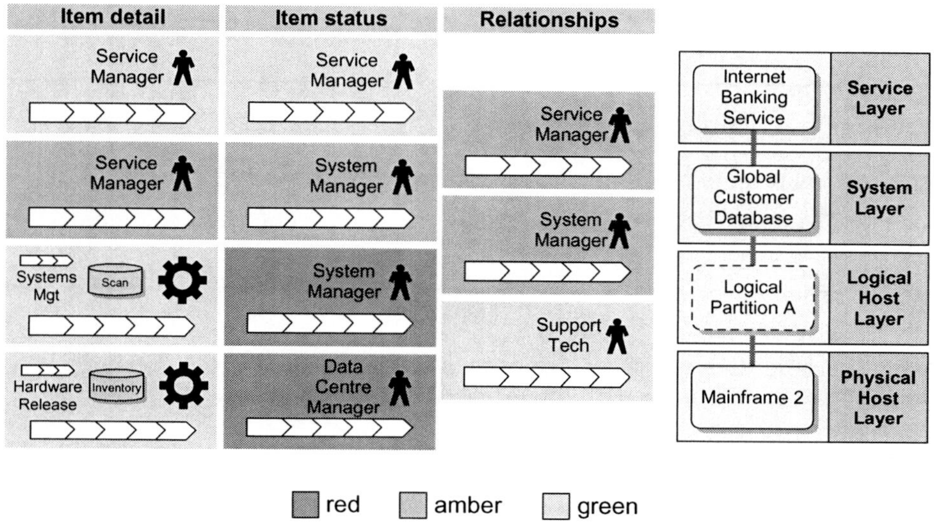

| | red | | amber | | green |

Davison went on to cover an approach that delegates could use to evaluate their own process framework and maturity based on seven categories of questions that should be identified as red, amber or green as shown in Table 10.1.

**Table 10.1** Process and maturity evaluation

| Assessment category | Question |
| --- | --- |
| Objective | Is your objective clear? (i.e. Have you designed your data model and specified your data sources?) |
| Data ownership | Do you have clear accountability for data ownership? |
| Documentation | Do you have maps and text for all elements of your process framework? |
| Training and support | Have you trained all key stakeholders and supported them with job aids, storyboards etc.? |
| Measures and metrics | Do you have metrics and key performance indicators (KPIs) in place that define how your process is performing? |

*(Continued)*

**Table 10.1** *(Continued)*

| Assessment category | Question |
| --- | --- |
| Adherence and control | Does someone police adherence to the process? |
| Continual improvement | Do you capture process risks and issues? |
| | Do you continuously drive improvement in the process? |

Delegates could then run their processes, perhaps manually, past the same checklist, again ending up with areas prioritised for attention.

At the end of all this analysis, delegates should come up with a new process in which the required data and the data actually delivered by the automated system are the same and the waste associated with various ad hoc handovers and the manual management of service variation request forms is eliminated.

Nevertheless, designing and implementing a new process is not easy. It is useful to identify key inhibitors to delivering a new process that need to be managed as part of an improvement project. Illustrative examples are:

- process engineering skills might be coloured red, needing the provision of formal training in the general principles of what makes a good process, and the methodology of process development;
- process notation skills might be coloured amber because of a lack of experience of different process notations, for varying levels of detail, and various audiences;
- measures and metrics skills might be coloured red because of a lack of formal training on identifying and implementing meaningful metrics and measures;
- a transient user base might be coloured amber because the owners of change are a constantly changing population, which makes them partially anonymous and non-accountable, and low-skilled in terms of CMDB;
- training facilities might be coloured green because rooms and equipment needed for user training are hard to come by, but this issue is being actively addressed.

The combination of process improvement and identification of key inhibitors to the establishment of an effective process leads to the development of an action plan for 'what I'm going to do tomorrow'. So, for example, you might have planned actions to:

- learn process engineering with formal training in the methodology of process development – and the current status of this might be coloured red;

- research the use of different process notations by gathering existing process documentation used in your organisation and searching Google® images for 'Process Map', perhaps selecting the bits you like from all the differing formats available – and the current status of this might also be coloured red;

- learn all about metrics and KPIs by taking formal training in the general principles of what makes a good process, and how to establish meaningful measures – and the current status of this might be coloured amber because training is scheduled and the trainers booked;

- learn how to develop storyboards by experimenting with storyboards and job aids, with a view to helping to step users through the tricky aspects of the process and using screenshots to make it visual – this might also be coloured amber because the research process has started.

Delegates then tried to build their own action plans for the scenarios of which they had personal experience.

## CONTRIBUTORS TO THE INTERACTIVE SESSION

Thirty-five contributors to the discussion represented the practitioner community. They included representatives from Principia IT, Cheshire County Council, TfL, Staffordshire Police, Renault UK, Mouchel, BAE, JPMorganChase, Plymouth City Council, Allen & Overy, Haringey Council, HM Land Registry, FireScope Europe, Friends Provident, iQuate, May Gurney Ltd, Cargill PLC, University of Oxford, GSK, KPMG, Mediatek Wireless, Ernst & Young Global, Atos Origin, EDS, HMPS, ING Bank (NL), Unilever, Motability Operations and Moore Stephens.

## PARTICIPATING PRACTITIONER COMMUNITY FEEDBACK

The delegates were first asked to consider the question 'Where are the gaps or weaknesses in your process or data/information?'. The answers were collated using the interactive technology under the following categories:

- Identification – data type = Service
- Identification – data type = System
- Identification – data type = Logical host layer
- Identification – data type = Hardware/physical host layer
- Identification – data type = Other
- Categorisation – Details
- Categorisation – Status
- Categorisation – Relationships
- Categorisation – Other

### Identification – data type = Service

Identifying services at the top level was an issue, especially becuase the business does not always know what its own services are. Understanding exactly what a service is can be a problem because you may not have service contracts for each service. Service definitions vary according to whom you talk: operations managers, service delivery managers, users, all have different definitions and requirements for different levels of item detail.

Delegates had difficulty in understanding who the users of each service are, in identifying internal services and establishing ownership for them, in mapping devices to services (which may be high priority but is hard to automate).

Identifying service relationships and maintaining them and the associated ownership data was reported as an issue, as was the maintenance of reporting relationships (understanding which specific business users to inform concerning downtime or service availability).

### Identification – data type = System

Delegates identified one likely and fundamental issue for automation here: that they do not have agents running on all servers. Sometimes particular server platforms do not support the agent technology (perhaps they are obsolete platforms for which there is no business case for an upgrade). Limited access to legacy and complex systems often means that coverage of the full estate is extremely difficult and sometimes hardware is logged locally, perhaps in the data centre (probably in a spreadsheet) and other teams do not have sight of it. For whatever reason, having a complete asset inventory is something you cannot achieve, even (perhaps especially) with automated discovery.

Naming standards can be an issue too, as can identifying the business services supported by your systems and deciding what is included in them: different areas of the business and various technology groups may use different terms for the same things, and service definitions may overlap. Identifying accurate lists for applications and their status and owners is often difficult, and identification of system owners can be especially fraught. Even deciding what exactly is 'a system' can be an issue.

However, tracking software (only a subset of what is needed) may be easier if an organisation has recognised the issue of software compliance (a software licence audit may be planned).

### Identification – data type = Logical host layer

Controlling virtualisation was identified as an issue here (for example sometimes VMware® servers automatically move from server farm to server farm). Ownership of services as opposed to ownership of systems could be another issue and delegates thought that these issues might manifest themselves when the organisation tried to use its configuration data to support maintenance of business continuity.

### Identification – data type = Hardware/physical host layer

Lack of automated processes can be a challenge because it can be resource intensive and getting staff to follow processes is difficult. The hardware catalogue is often one big bucket of different server and network repositories without a centralised location for holding physical assets. Nevertheless, automation has its issues too, such as tracking the installation of agents, making agents work over the internet, and tracking virtualised services across physical servers.

Automated import of desktop hardware information can be easy enough, but location by IP address or services used is difficult, and this may always be necessary.

Integration of information about servers, switches, links, printers etc., held in different files and tool formats can be an issue. One delegate said, 'Our tool has to get at this via export from our management system to Excel®, then by importing Excel® CSV format, so relationships get lost.'

### Identification – data type = Other
You need to identify software and software versions running on the server estate, of course, but sometimes a client requires items like PDAs to be captured, which can be difficult to maintain. Maintenance is an issue: you have to decide which CIs to record data for, on a basis of, 'if you want it, how are you going to maintain it?'.

Relationships can be tricky too, where (for example) a CI is dependent on multiple CIs but not necessarily all at the same time, such as when this server or that server must be up but both don't need to be up at the same time.

### Categorisation – Details
As usual, data quality and data accuracy were fundamental issues. One delegate said, 'We don't have good attribute information or aren't sure information is correct.' With outsourced infrastructure, where some items are controlled by third parties, a lack of confidence in the quality of data is quite common. You need a way to coordinate audits of all details both outsourced and in-house.

You need to be able to identify critical applications and decide on ownership and governance, and use this to help to prioritise understanding and definition of a CI and attribute level that will appeal to and work for both IT and the business. You should anticipate possible conflict over system and service categorisation by business area, function or personal opinion. As always, the CMS team needs good people and negotiation skills.

### Categorisation – Status
This can be a significant challenge. If a CI is owned by business users its status may often be effectively unknown (this is an issue to address, not a desirable state of affairs). You need to record the status of changes against each application as well as knowing the status of assets such as servers, workstations and facilities.

The decommissioning process can also be a challenge, especially with automated discovery: has a CI been decommissioned or has its host simply been switched off? There is a tendency not to remove things from the CMDB in case they are only temporarilly absent, although perhaps they should be recorded as 'retired' (but then, do you want to distinguish between 'scrapped', 'disposed of/sold' and 'stolen'?). You need to think of decommissioning as a process and decide what information is worth keeping and why.

Sometimes the status of assets is not clear, for example is something truly operational or just a 'functional demonstrator', perhaps for a proof of concept?

It is important to think about when the status of assets is determined: there is a relationship with the change or problem management process.

### Categorisation – Relationships

Identifying dependencies between applications, hardware and people can be difficult, as can identifying an authoritative source for this information. There are few, if any, tools to help with this and understanding the implications of incorrectly defining relationships is important. Even understanding which is which in a parent–child relationship can be non-trivial. Investment is needed to determine and document relationships, and then there is the challenge of controlling and managing this information going forward. There is also the issue of knowing when all the relationships are defined: knowing when to stop (which is partly why working with a structured framework is useful). You are finished when all stakeholders are happy that their needs have been met.

Relationships with customised objects can be especially difficult to identify and maintain.

People issues are particularly important: a lot of relationship information is in people's heads (and it can be difficult to get rid of a dependency on heroes and tacit knowledge in people's heads). Often, the CMDB is viewed as an asset database only and people don't understand the importance of defining and maintaining relationships. Identifying roles within human resource systems and business continuity plans can aid user administration and provide imports of relationship information for the CMDB. Roles can be important to relationships between assets and facilities too. One delegate mentioned the operations team having to operate without their laptops during a fire: the service had to continue, and you need to keep track of business services and the infrastructure they run or rely on.

### Categorisation – Other

Delegates confirmed several general issues:

- Measuring the wrong things, such as measuring performance not business outputs.

- Allowing the CM tool to drive the process.

- Senior management bypassing controls/process to shoehorn in changes to meet the 'business need' (but perhaps there should be a formally documented 'emergency change' process).

- Not understanding the importance of cultural change as complementing the introduction of a CMDB tool.

- Not clearly identifying the 'master repository' for data when the CMDB is taking data from another application.

### Weaknesses in process or data/information from real life

Delegates were asked to consider the top three weaknesses in their approach to maintaining their CMDB from the following list:

- Objective – unclear (7 votes);
- Data ownership – unclear accountability for data ownership (20 votes);
- Documentation – lack of maps and text (12 votes);
- Training and support – inadequate (6 votes);
- Measures and metrics – lack of process metrics/KPIs (13 votes);
- Adherence and control – lack of policing (24 votes);
- Continuous improvement – risks/issues/improvements not driven (2 votes);
- Other (4 votes).

The results are presented in Figure 10.4. The importance of anticipating, identifying and addressing any data ownership issues in existing processes is clear. Delegates also identified politics and the existence of processes allowing change outside the domain of the CMDB as being general issues around populating their CMDB (although some delegates thought that their biggest barrier to populating their CMDB was that they hadn't finished designing it yet!).

### Key inhibitors and mitigating actions
This session finished with an attempt to identify the key inhibitors the delegates actually encounter, and to document some actions taken to address these inhibitors. In no particular order, the inhibitors reported were:

**Figure 10.4** Weaknesses in your process or data/information?

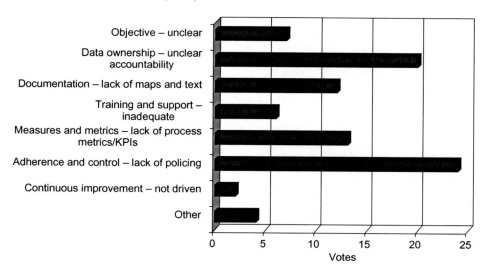

- A lack of informed management buy-in or commitment, from the right people. There may be no management vision for the role of configuration management or buy-in to ITIL as a standard. There may be a lack of understanding of the value of the CMDB (or, indeed, the CMS generally), with CMDB maintenance perceived as being just more bureaucracy. Conversely, there may be too much micromanagement by top-level management (the wrong sort of buy-in) and not enough input from staff who know what's really going on and actually do the job!

- Poor project management.
- A lack of money or assigned budget for configuration management.
- An unsupportive or dysfunctional company culture especially in global organisations, where there may well be no one way of doing things, globally. This often manifests itself as resistance to change or, at least, to being changed (as one delegate said, 'Long-standing members of the department can be set in their ways.')
- A lack of knowledge and experience around process engineering, a lack of institutionalised process, a lack of methods of introducing better process and a lack of skills and resources (time and people) generally, especially in the service delivery team.
- A lack of enforcement for process conformance.

Delegates thought that the management buy-in and cultural issues could be addressed by understanding what services the CMS provides to the business, and persuading stakeholders to get involved in defining the services that will benefit them. If you really understand the business process, you may be able to come up with novel solutions that add real value or comfort. At least one delegate thought that they would be able to present a proposal based on what they are learning from this CMSG/itSMF conference and use it to gain buy-in from clients.

Matching user requirements with the capabilities of the CMS and good process documentation is important (and remember that different audiences will need their own localised variations, possibly in their own language). You must identify key stakeholders and what they require and prioritise delivery of this. You cannot do it all at once. Getting input and buy-in from developers is also important.

Stakeholders may have resource issues with their existing workload. The CM team can summarise the relevant arguments and document the anticipated/delivered benefits, so that stakeholders have a snapshot of progress against plan, and simple options that enable them to make 'go/no go' decisions.

Enforcement of the CM process and maintenance of the CMS is a challenge. Non-conformance by individuals should be openly visible to aid peer enforcement (but take care to avoid any appearance of a witch-hunt against people who do not, cannot or will not 'get' the CMS). The availability of training can be a great help by teaching good practice and this is much more effective than trying to punish those who do not use good practice. Management conformance can be promoted by including configuration management in a balanced scorecard approach.

## CONCLUSION

This session was very popular and many delegates from many organisations across different sectors attended it. Its title *How do you populate your CMDB?* clearly identified a pain point for many practitioners. It covers many of the aspects that organisations and practitioners need to consider when designing and improving their data/information and process in a way that enables maintenance of the information.

Davison designed the interactive session around a sample CMDB structure, data source framework and process framework. His aim was to identify ways of improving a current process framework using gap analysis techniques and to explore ways of improving the process.

By starting with the identification of configuration items, their information, states and relationships, delegates found it easy to get a picture of the overall scope of configuration management and understand the key roles involved in maintaining the information in the samples Davison provided. The identification activities were based on the ITIL configuration identification activities, summarised in Chapter 1, and included:

- identifying the configuration model;
- identifying the assets and CIs to be managed, their attributes, associated documentation;
- identifying relationships between CIs.

Clearly identifying the roles that are responsible for maintaining the items' details, items' status and relationships between items helps to engage the right people, those that can really help to improve the process and data/information.

The approach that Davison used in this session can be applied in a workshop session for any organisation because it works well: participants are learning throughout the session and engaged. In our experience, this general approach can be used as the basis of an improvement workshop for configuration management. For example:

1 Present a sample CMDB structure with item information.

2 Present the existing process framework (with examples).

3 Undertake an initial gap analysis: identify the gaps or weaknesses in your process or data/information.

4 Present an example of process engineering: take an existing process and eliminate redundant or frustrating activities to simplify and streamline the process. This should enable participants to aim for significant improvements.

5 Complete the gap analysis: identify more gaps or weaknesses in your process or data/information.

6 Brainstorm: identify and prioritise your key inhibitors to establishing effective process.

7 Brainstorm: identify and prioritise key actions you feel would overcome these inhibitors and produce an action plan ('What will I do differently tomorrow?').

The session demonstrated the importance of understanding the scope and key CI types to be controlled by configuration management early because it helps people understand the overall picture they can work from during the gap analysis and improvement discussions.

# 11 IMPLEMENTATION

## OBJECTIVE

The objective of this chapter is to explore a variety of different approaches to bringing the CMS to fruition.

## SUMMARY

Time constraints meant that discussion of this issue was limited to a strategic view of the CMS architecture, the design and the build processes.

Four approaches to integrating existing configuration files into a holistic CMS were considered:

- In-house integration;
- External systems integration;
- A primary supplier (vendor) solution;
- A hybrid of all of these.

## BRINGING THE CMS TO FRUITION

This section is based on a presentation by Mark Bools of Principia IT. Bools has over 20 years' experience helping organisations to optimise the management of their IT systems. Starting as a software engineer in 1987 and moving swiftly through management to freelance consulting he has both a strong technical and managerial background, providing clients with the best of both worlds.

Bools started as a software engineer working first on expert systems, then real-time systems. He soon moved into project management and then configuration management. For the past 20 years he has been involved with configuration management for large and small organisations, on projects, programmes and at the corporate strategic level. He has developed solutions for organisations as diverse as Barclays Bank, AMP, British Midlands Airways, East Midlands Electricity, GMAC-RFC, UK Passport Office and National Savings. He has also provided consultancy for some of the leading CM tool vendors, among them Serena and Continuus Software (now IBM).

Bools challenged the assembled delegates to think about what the CMS actually is and what they want it to achieve, starting from the basic definition of the CMS in the ITIL glossary:

†"A set of tools and databases that are used to manage an IT Service Provider's Configuration data. The CMS also includes information about incidents, problems, known errors, changes and releases; and may contain data about employees, suppliers, locations, business units, customers and users. The CMS includes tools for collecting, storing, managing, updating, and presenting data about all Configuration Items and their Relationships. The CMS is maintained by configuration management and is used by all IT service management processes."

The CMS is also a foundation for IT governance and even corporate governance generally. We think that if you do not know what you have, where it is, who is responsible for it and how it is configured, then you cannot claim any sort of governance. As Tom DeMarco once famously exclaimed, 'You cannot control what you cannot measure.' Without an effective CMS, even something as fundamental as security is undermined.

Obviously there was too much here to cover in one interactive session, so Bools limited the discussion to a strategic view of the CMS architecture, the design process and the build process.

Bools asked delegates to consider where to start from and suggested the following possible starting points:

- Auditing your current assets databases, spreadsheets, purchase information and development databases.
- Identifying which business and service management processes the CMS is to support.
- Identifying the roles that require access to the system. This affects all manner of decisions from authentication, how people get access to the system, how people are removed, the different ways of accessing the system (through a single front-end or several front-ends, locally or remotely, and so on).

### Architecture
With regards to architecture, ITIL provides an architectural model for the CMS that is part of the Service Knowledge Management System (see Figure 11.1 and the overview in Chapter 1). Bools used the CMS architecture to set the scene and asked delegates to consider all the layers of the CMS architecture:

- †"Presentation layer;
- Knowledge processing layer;
- Information integration layer;
- Data and information sources (individual)."

**Figure 11.1** CMS architectural model [Based on figure in OGC Service Transition ISBN 978-0-113310-48-7]

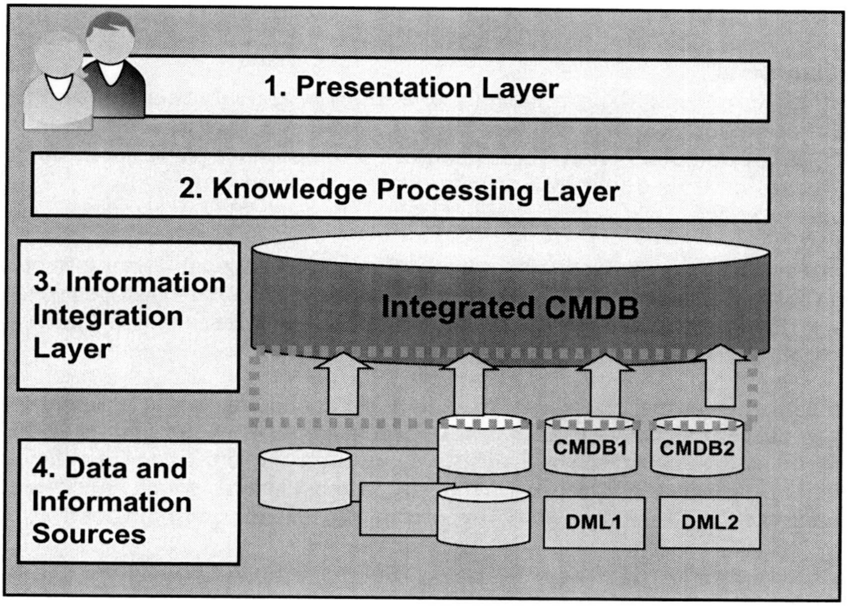

In order to deliver the information integration layer there must be applications and integrations that operate across the individual data and information sources, and which deliver information to the information integration layer. These include:

- common schemes, process, data and information;
- mapping schemas;
- managing metadata;
- data reconciliation;
- data synchronisation;
- extract, load, transform functions;
- data mining.

The information architecture of the CMS is important and this should be driven by the scope of the CI types, the naming and identification standards. You will need to decide what data is to be held for each CI. The configuration item types used as examples in ITIL were presented:

- †"Service Lifecycle CIs;
- Service CIs;
- Organisation CIs;

- Internal CIs;
- External CIs;
- Interface CIs."

### Design and build

You will need to think about provisioning a solution and whether this will be in-house or outsourced. You will also need to decide whether to adopt an evolutionary implementation (this is usually recommended) or a revolutionary implementation (this might be a possible choice if you're starting from scratch with a new team).

Don't overlook business continuity because the CMS is probably going to be mission critical (it needs to be backed up), but think about the restore process and how timely it can or needs to be, and about the resilience of CMS processes and procedures in the event of disaster or less extreme contingencies.

In a contingency situation (which, in some CMS scenarios, might simply be changing outsourcer) is your data readily recoverable? Can the system be in/outsourced easily? In outsourced situations be careful to consider both the technical and contractual issues surrounding the ease with which changes can be made to the arrangement. And, are you tied to specific technologies?

The different options for integration also need to be considered. These include:

- in-house integration;
- external systems integration;
- a primary supplier (vendor) solution;
- a hybrid of all of these.

### A practical view

The delegates' views, based on their practical experience, were recorded with the aid of the interactive technology.

## CONTRIBUTORS TO THE INTERACTIVE SESSION

Seventeen contributors to the discussion represented the practitioner community. They included representatives from ING Bank (NL), Staffordshire Police, DeltaRail Group Limited, Met Office, Mouchel, Haringey Council, BAE Systems, FireScope, BAA, Plymouth City Council, Nottingham Trent University and Motability Operations.

## PARTICIPATING PRACTITIONER COMMUNITY FEEDBACK

### Ranking the different approaches

Looking at the question 'Which of the following strategic approaches would be most suitable for your organisation to achieve an integrated CMS?', the options chosen were:

- Do not need one (no votes);
- In-house integration (4 votes);
- External systems integration (no votes);
- Primary supplier integration (6 votes);
- Hybrid (8 votes);
- Don't know (2 votes).

These results are shown in Figure 11.2.

**Figure 11.2** Strategic approaches

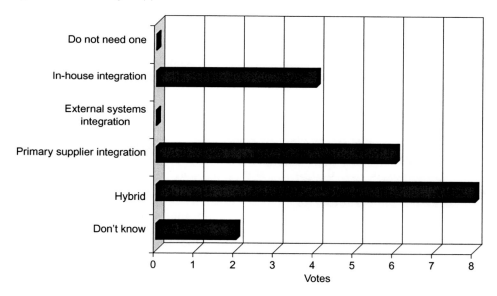

It is interesting, but perhaps not surprising, that a hybrid combination of all the integration options (a chosen vendor, external systems integrator and in-house integration) seems to be the preferred option.

**Practical requirements for the different approaches**
Delegates were then asked to consider each strategic approach and respond to the question 'What are the key requirements (for each approach) to achieve an integrated CMS?'. Their output was captured via the interactive technology.

In-house integration
According to the delegates, it obviously helps if everything in the CMS is all on one platform, or at least on a multi-platform infrastructure that provides equal capabilities for all platforms and allows the free interchange of information across all platforms. If the CMS is limited to a particular technology platform, integrating CMS processes that need to run in incompatible technology silos will be harder.

Producing a fully integrated CMS needs to be treated as an entire lifecycle development project, with long-term financial support and resources and sufficient capabilities in-house to deliver the solution. You must understand the problem and scope the requirements before starting, which includes understanding the scope of integration. Consider and understand the total cost of ownership, including the cost of keeping the knowledge of how it all works within easy reach through properly maintained documentation and training of operators, those responsible for day-to-day operation of the CMS and maintainers, and those responsible for maintaining and developing the CMS supporting applications and infrastructure. Using in-house resources is often more cost-effective than the alternatives expanded below providing you have the specialist skills and trained personnel available and can ensure that all involved are working towards an agreed objective.

You should ensure that you set realistic timescales, establish common naming conventions, produce good-quality documentation and make adequate and supportive tools available. Stakeholders need to be identified and involved from the start and good project management, which can collaborate with the in-house technical team, is vital.

You must have a good business case and business sponsorship from a point high enough in the organisation to be effective. You must achieve buy-in to the finally agreed scope, which might end up as a compromise and might have to 'multilayer' the available views: so, for example, several Operational Services might be linked to form a User Service, and perhaps email, plus Citrix®, plus web access, plus an Office Suite might be linked to form a Standard Desktop Service.

### External systems integration
Delegates thought that clear objectives and requirements, with good project management, are especially important if you are going on this route. You'll need a really clear understanding of the systems to be integrated (and good descriptions of them). You'll need to follow standard project management procedures as well as normal Development, Testing, Acceptance and Production (DTAP) project phases, with a clear definition of the outputs required. You must have a clear definition to which the external agency can work.

You'll need to establish, in your requirements, what you need to know now and anticipate what you might require in the future. Test managers should be involved from the start. You'll need a clear statement of the processes involved and you'll want to involve key users and their management right from the beginning, together with experienced people from your project team.

Once again, the business case and sponsorship at a high enough management level is important and normal project management good practice applies: SLAs, requirements etc. Think big, start small: dig deep first, then widen the scope, thus ensuring that you retain in-house control of the work effort.

There are other special issues to consider when using external system integrators, such as ensuring that there is adequate training of in-house staff and effective knowledge transfer at the end of the project. You won't want to end up with a system that you can't support because it uses standards and terminology foreign to your organisation, so you should implement a common data dictionary and ruthlessly rationalise the data against that dictionary. Your requirements should include a clear glossary of terms that the external system integrator must conform to when writing documentation and preparing training. Any submission from the external integrator should be validated against your organisation's standards and existing terminology, in order to ensure consistency.

You should also be prepared to accept guidance from the external organisation. If you can't trust what it is telling you, why are you employing them?

### Primary supplier integration

The first requirement here, delegates thought, is that you have a flexible and well-established primary supplier, with well-supported tools. You must have clear contractual agreements with your supplier, including KPIs, SLAs etc., and OLAs within internal operational teams. You should carry out thorough due diligence on the vendor and its market position, understand its outlook for the future and ensure that it is consistent with your organisation's strategic objectives.

You will need at least some in-house technical and business experience in order to work with the supplier to get what the business really needs, and make sure that an ongoing training programme for the new technology is included. You don't want to get into the situation where the supplier can hold you to ransom because you don't have the in-house skills needed to operate and manage its solution.

However, the main issue here is 'trust': who is in control, you or your supplier? At least one delegate's reaction to this scenario was 'I'm not convinced this will ever work.'

### Hybrid

In this approach, some of the work is done in-house and some by an external party (whether by a systems integrator or by a primary supplier). This approach demands significantly more management finesse because, in addition to managing the programme of work undertaken by each contributor, the coordination between the parties must also be very carefully managed to ensure that requirements are not overlooked and that each of the constituent solutions integrate as a whole. We think that this means that the issues pertaining to all the various options probably apply, together with the additional risk that things could fall into the cracks between them.

Delegates agreed that you must define the CMS/CMDB project scope and deliverables particularly clearly in this situation. Often, the manual effort for mapping what you have currently onto what you are going to have in the final implementation and maintaining business continuity while you are introducing the new CMS approach isn't factored into the budget. This means that you run out of money and the project is either stopped (which is at least a controllable state of affairs) or proceeds unsteadily in a compromised form, with significant costs and little real benefit. 'No wonder,' as one delegate commented, 'that 70 per cent of worldwide CMDB projects fail.'

If you take this approach, you'll either need a very good federated CMDB technology with a good integration portal or you'll need to make everybody use the same CMDB (which isn't really in the spirit of ITIL). Consolidating on a single CMDB will probably involve the additional complexity and cost of a separate data import project.

You'll need a clear set of agreed standards and processes to ensure that the different parties work together. Nevertheless, estimating costs and ROI, building an integrated CMS architecture (based on the functional requirements you've identified for your environment) and delivering it, and then demonstrating a real ROI, will still be a challenge.

Best practices from ITIL will help, but these are expressed at quite a high level and delegates thought that customers would still struggle to define their detailed functional requirements: it's not always clear where they should go to discover detailed best practices for, for example, exactly what a 'forward schedule of change report' should include. The answer, perhaps, is to use the CM community: the CMSG networking events, itSMF events, CM Crossroads (which is starting to develop a CM Body of Knowledge) and ITIL Live.

## CONCLUSION

It is interesting, we think, that the feedback on this session was less well structured and less defined than that from other sessions. Perhaps people were so focused on the main journey that the final stages don't get the attention that they should.

It is clear that controlling the whole CMS project in-house was seen as a bit of a luxury by most delegates and that relying on a prime technology supplier was viewed with some mistrust. And, we were pleased to see that handing over the whole thing to an external SI isn't very popular: a CMS needs to be something you do at least partly for yourself, not have imposed on you (you could achieve this if you have a good, properly managed, relationship with a external SI, but experience suggests that such relationships are not common in practice).

It is no surprise that the majority (although not an overwhelming majority) of delegates preferred a hybrid approach, with significant work done in-house, and we are pleased that the risks associated with this approach seem to be recognised. These are integration and communications risks, and they are addressed by running the CMS project as a proper project, adequately budgeted for and with enforcement of agreed standards and processes. And a good federated CMDB technology helps too.

Nevertheless, we feel that there is a further aspect of bringing the CMS to fruition that wasn't really brought out by delegates. This is that the true fruition of a CMS project is its use to support 'all the ITIL process owners, service owners, service management, service operations and IT staff' (see Chapter 1, page 4). That is, it needs to be used, actively, to support people's service management activities, and it is as much to do with decision support as it is to do with what we think of as technical management of configuration. A CMS, we think, really comes to fruition when the business sees itself as a stakeholder and uses it to help it make business decisions. To this end, we think that an increased emphasis on the involvement of the business in the establishment of the CMDB is beneficial. Procuring continual business support for such a significant enterprise requires that the business stakeholders see the purpose and direct benefit to themselves throughout.

This is a matter of perspective. The CMS doesn't really come to fruition just when the CMDB gets implemented and data gets put into it. It comes to fruition when the CMS is institutionalised as part of 'the way we do things here'. Which means, in turn, that you shouldn't assess the success or otherwise of your implementation too early. You should provide continuing support for 'bedding in' the CMS after the initial technology implementation and you should schedule the post-implementation review (PIR) for after it has been in production use for a while. This implies that budget should be available for addressing any issues identified in the post implementation. If there are issues with your implementation, the worst outcome is that resources aren't available to address them and (see the delegates' feedback, above) the CMS 'proceeds unsteadily in a compromised form, with significant costs and little real benefit'.

It is also vitally important that the maintenance of the CMS is anticipated. It is common, particularly when business support is not properly acquired and a 'bedding in' warranty period is not correctly planned, for the CMS to degrade and become distrusted by its users. This distrust leads to misuse and consequent failure of the entire CMS enterprise, often at significant cost.

# 12 GOOD IDEAS... AND ONES TO AVOID

## OBJECTIVES

Many IT organisations find it difficult to implement configuration management for various reasons. This chapter identifies what works and what doesn't work for the implementation of configuration management and the CMS.

## SUMMARY

This chapter surveys and summarises what works, what doesn't work and how you measure success, with input not only from experienced presenters, but also from the assembled practitioners gathered in an interactive session. By identifying the implementation challenges and barriers you will be able to develop effective implementation strategies to avoid them and so reduce the risk of failure.

## WHAT WORKS AND WHAT DOES NOT

This section is based on a presentation by Shirley Lacy (of ConnectSphere) and Ian Salvage (then of IBM).

The foundation for any CMS implementation is well-trained people, who have the right information and good technology-enabled processes to enable delivery of quality services to the business, as shown in Figure 12.1.

---

**Figure 12.1** Service environment

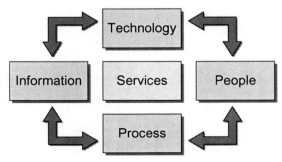

The presenters suggested that the following factors are critical for a successful implementation.

- Programme/project implementation factors:

    o A realistic, agreed scope and objectives;

    o A structured, planned implementation with tight project management;

    o The selection of partners and consultants to help to deliver the vision;

    o An informed executive commitment and active senior management sponsorship;

    o A clear communication of benefits to stakeholders;

    o Getting the process owner and all stakeholders actively engaged in the project.

- Process, tools and automation and people factors:

    o A structured approach based on accepted standards and frameworks such as ITIL, COBIT®, ISO/IEC 20000;

    o Documented policies and clearly defined roles and responsibilities;

    o Documented process flows;

    o A clear process for audit and reconciliation;

    o A seamless integration of other business processes with configuration management;

    o An effective and integrated service management tool or application;

    o Integrated asset discovery tools.

- People with service management skills.

What, in their experience, doesn't work well is a project approach with:

- a large initial scope and unclear objectives;
- unrealistic expectations for ROI;
- islands of fragmented effort;
- insufficient process design effort;
- inadequate planning (i.e. not considering the full breadth of work and organisational change required);
- a lack of integration of people, process, technology and data;
- an insufficient consideration of possible dependencies on other projects;
- a poor tool selection process;
- a lack of executive commitment, or the wrong sort of (uninformed or micromanaged) executive commitment.

The interactive session then attempted to determine, using the experience of the assembled delegates, what needs to be added to these lists, whether there were any issues with any of the items listed, and whether they can be grouped to assist in implementation.

## CONTRIBUTORS TO THE INTERACTIVE SESSION

Twenty contributors to the discussion represented the practitioner community. They included representatives from Met Office, Mentor IT Ltd, GlaxoSmithKline, ATSC, DeltaRail Group, Haringey Council, University of Oxford, EDS, Eracent, May Gurney Ltd., Fidelity Investments, Bytes, O2, DHL, Plymouth City Council, and Prudential.

## PARTICIPATING PRACTITIONER COMMUNITY FEEDBACK

At the start of the interactive session, delegates were asked to repeat a previous vote, picking up to three stakeholders (from the stakeholder list in Chapter 3) that would benefit the most from the CMS. Each person voted individually using the interactive technology and the results were displayed immediately on the main screen for comment (see Figure 12.2).

**Figure 12.2** Key stakeholders

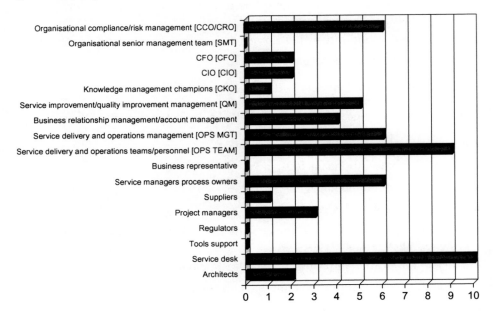

The most important stakeholders are thought to be the service desk, service delivery and operations teams, compliance and risk managers, service managers and process owners.

## What works?
Delegates were invited to consider 'what works' for these stakeholders in particular, under eight headings:

- Scope and objectives;
- Journey/approach;
- Service asset and CM process;
- Sponsors and stakeholders;
- Organisation, people and culture;
- CMS solution;
- Integration;
- Other.

### What works: scope and objectives
Carefully defining a limited, achievable scope, which is agreed by all the relevant parties at the beginning, is crucial.

Try to balance the need to avoid changing the scope against responding to changing requirements as stakeholders gain better understanding of what is involved.

Be very clear about what you are trying to achieve and what decisions and processes you need the CMS to support. 'It is important to think both for tomorrow and today,' delegates said, 'but you must manage expectations and incremental delivery.'

Be very clear about what can be delivered in the short term and avoid trying 'to change the whole world in one go'. It is usually best to identify critical areas of the business or areas with particularly painful issues and work on these first because this delivers the most immediate buy-in: 'start small, scale fast, aim high'.

A clear scope and objectives helps to 'get sufficient budget for people, time and money'.

It is important to have leaders who can 'visualise the holistic solution and who can position manageable pieces of the whole'. One delegate said, 'Take a top-down approach and always keep the problem you are trying to solve in view. Without this understanding you will stray badly.'

### What doesn't work: scope and objectives
Try to avoid making assumptions. For example, assuming that buy-in from one part of the organisation will result in adoption by the rest of the organisation.

The implementation will fail if you do not consult with all the stakeholders early, even if the implementation for some of the stakeholders follows later on in the project journey. Remember that 'one person (or IT silo) driving the project and setting the scope to match their own needs can alienate all the other potential stakeholders'.

You need to 'avoid storing data simply because you have it; always ask what value it adds to the CMS, and for whom'.

You will fail if you try to 'boil the ocean' or set too ambitious a scope (without incremental 'small wins' on the way). On the other hand, setting too narrow a scope can be fatal too.

### What works: the journey and approach generally
The end point can affect the journey, so try to achieve business-focused consensus on a clear expected end result, and define your success factors early on.

Standard team-building and personal management techniques work. For example have a 'firewalled' team of two or three people who are allowed to question, raise concerns, state that the project is off track and so on, without any fear of retribution. A small cooperative team with dedicated time will work better than a part-time team with a day job to do, and make sure that you have competent process representatives and domain experts on the project team.

The tools you choose will influence the journey, choose them carefully and learn how to use them so there are no surprises downstream. On the other hand, you must spend a reasonable time defining your requirements and testing them with users before you select your tools.

Define measures that prove the journey is worthwhile before you start and demonstrate business benefits as milestones are reached. Show benefits to all stakeholders to encourage buy-in and cooperation. As one delegate said, 'How do you eat an elephant? Make sure you know what an elephant looks like, then take small easy bites at a time.' In other words do not expect the journey to proceed in a straight line without sustenance on the way. In addition, consider adopting an 'evangelistic approach': grow champions who will grow further champions...

### What doesn't work: the journey and approach generally
Delegates suggested that what doesn't work is 'trying to railroad the project through without consultation and buy-in by everyone involved'. 'Simply holding large evangelical conferences to achieve buy-in will not work either. No matter how good your evangelists are, your workforce has seen it before and simply won't believe them unless practical benefits are achieved quickly.' If people do not experience real benefits you will never get buy-in. It is also important to avoid taking a big bang approach 'by promising the world and delivering nothing until after everyone has lost interest in the project'.

### What works: service asset and configuration management process
What works is making sure that your process and its purpose are clearly defined. You will need 'fit for purpose' automation and tools. It is important to identify the

correct level of CI, at a low enough level to be useful but not so low as to present a maintenance nightmare.

Walking through scenarios of the process in action will help to ensure its validity. Try to involve the end users of the system in the process, by including reporting/dashboard capabilities they can use, and by looking at both current process and their wish lists.

Most important, keep it simple, with minimal bureaucracy!

### What doesn't work: service asset and configuration management process
What won't work is 'assuming that CMS tools will fix a currently broken process' or that 'realms of documentation, gathering dust' achieve anything. Automating bad process does not work, it simply results in the wrong things being done faster and less flexibly.

Another good route to failure is writing 'training materials in obscure technical language'. Giving people a way to circumvent the process or tools is also a bad idea.

### What works: sponsors and stakeholders
Get the buy-in and involvement of the people who really know the business and benefit from the process. 'In our case, our service desk personnel have been invaluable in reminding us of the reality,' one delegate volunteered. Another pointed out that 'the lowly front-line are the people that are going to be doing most of the work, even if they aren't paying for it directly, so their buy-in is vital'. However, you also need a senior sponsor that can help to avoid departmental politics. Ideally, this will be someone at CIO level or with multiple direct reports, including both IT service management and critical business owners who depend on the IT services.

You can 'pick a star to hitch onto', perhaps, and get them on board. Someone with the ear of senior management and the respect of those below them. It is a good idea to 'find the business area with the biggest budget and sell the solution to them the hardest. It might be not be exactly aligned with their roadmap, but if they have the cash...'

### What doesn't work: sponsors and stakeholders
What doesn't work is 'confusing budget approver and sponsor, or getting a sponsor at the wrong organisational level'. If sponsors are not senior enough 'it can take a couple of years of costly effort before real benefits are delivered'. However, at a lower level 'getting buy-in from IT engineers can be an uphill struggle too'.

On the other hand 'if the decision makers are dislocated from doers' you have too many stakeholders, or if the CMS project is technology-driven without focus on business (if you champion technical benefit as opposed to business process impact) you will also fail. And, 'sometimes stakeholders have their own agendas, do not see the bigger picture'.

### What works: organisation, people and culture

Networking and good communications at the individual level are vital and 'get users to buy-in – [dysfunctional] culture is your enemy'. So 'actually talk to people – broadcast emails do not work'. Ensure that people understand how the process benefits **them**. It is not your process, it's **our** process, so take time to understand how to make people cooperate. Delegates said, 'Emphasize that we are trying to help and allay fears about users losing control' and 'Show users the advantages of the new process/tool/whatever, with clear selling of benefits to users'. Aim for clear language, clear goals, clear objectives, working as a team, and definitely aim at not being seen as imposing something with no benefit.

### What doesn't work: organisation, people and culture

One delegate said, 'Don't be grumpy. Balance dictatorial with the touchy-feely. What you want is cooperative people working to the same goals rather than personal or sectional office agendas and political in-fighting.' And, of course, if outsourcers are used, make sure they use common processes and technology.

You can hinder organisation, people and cultural change by 'assuming that what you think of as a good idea is automatically seen as a good idea by everyone else', and by assuming that all the teams in the IT department will automatically cooperate. People with personal agendas (not seeing the bigger picture, not wearing the company hat) can sabotage things, sometimes unconsciously, sometimes because they concentrate on politics rather than results.

### What works: the CMS solution

The CMS solution should provide tight control and transparent information. Most vendor solutions do similar things, albeit in different ways, so do not spend too long on the selection, instead spend it on the implementation. Remember that 'good enough' delivers success with minimal overheads.

Delegates thought that you should look for an integrated tool for all the target areas in scope rather than buying separate tools and linking them. Try to choose a vendor that is a stable and responsive partner. Make sure that the GUI for any tool is very intuitive and user-friendly because the tool must support people's work activities to deliver benefits.

### What doesn't work: the CMS solution

Delegates said:

- 'Don't buy a solution that will not integrate with the rest of your service management tools.'

- 'Don't try to take everyone with you: you can never satisfy everyone.'

- 'Don't rely on sales pitches: make your own case based on a pilot.'

- 'Don't think that an off-the-shelf product that doesn't fit can be customised: take the best fit and live with its limitations.'

- 'Never give up update rights to everyone: good security or access control functionality is important.'

## What works: integration

It is best to integrate processes before tools and look for loosely coupled integration (i.e. using a web services API), so that components can be changed individually. Try to design in future extensibility because there will be new devices to manage during the lifetime of your CMS (e.g. blade servers and virtualisation).

Good configuration identification enables integration. Delegates emphasised, 'Integration will be a pain without clear naming standards.'

A good approach is to know what your outputs are, and then to map the information/data flows required to deliver these outputs.

## What doesn't work: integration

Delegates thought that integration is not worth considering for an immature organisation (e.g. one at CMMI® level 0) and that the following approaches will not work:

- Storing all data in a single database.
- Placing sole reliance on discovery tools.

## What works: other

The general advice is to apply common sense when all else fails, and to be resilient ('if you get knocked back, pick yourself up, rethink and go again').

Metrics are important. 'Fix the metrics early and ensure there are tension metrics.' Tension metrics are a set of related metrics in which improvements to one metric have a negative effect on another. Tension metrics are designed to ensure that an appropriate balance is achieved.

## Measuring success

The delegates then considered the question 'How can we measure success?', recording their ideas using the interactive technology.

The fundamental enabler for successful measurement was thought to be effective baselining: baseline the 'before' situation, then re-baseline at each milestone. Indicators are feedback from customer (stakeholder) satisfaction surveys with the tools, the change and configuration management processes, and timely sponsor and stakeholder sign-off at milestones.

## Tangible metrics and KPIs

Delegates identified more specific metrics and KPIs for consideration and noted that these metrics need to be reasonably straightforward to measure. Suggested metrics included:

- Metrics for better service and business performance:

  o A reduction in the number of service desk calls;
  o An increase in the first-time fix rate;

- o A decrease in mean time to service restoration;
- o Incidents fixed more quickly on services included in CMS;
- o A reduction in downtime;
- o An improvement in performance against benchmark;
- o A high service utilisation.

- Effectiveness and efficiency metrics for change and release management:
  - o Fewer failed changes as a result of incorrect configuration data or clashes on services covered by the CMS;
  - o A reduction in the number of reported incidents caused by change;
  - o Fewer changes required and better planned;
  - o Fewer releases per unit time with fewer bugs in them.

- Productivity metrics:
  - o Time needed to access the needed information;
  - o Cost reduction/avoidance metrics;
  - o A reduction in software licence costs from better software asset management and the aggregation of licences and associated reduction in fees;
  - o Hardware purchase costs should decrease as redundant IT is identified;
  - o A reduction in the number of service desk calls;
  - o A reduction in power costs;
  - o Better resource usage leading to lower capital expenditure;
  - o Fewer instances of changes requiring rework/second implementations;
  - o Better information should lower support staff training costs;
  - o More time charged to billable work, less time on service overheads.

- Risk and compliance metrics:
  - o A reduction in unauthorised changes;
  - o More compliance reports showing decreasing risk.

Possible intangible metrics to consider are:

- an improved visibility of relationships between systems and services leading to better impact analysis and cost allocation;
- an improved ability to predict problems;
- cost avoidance for upcoming projects by providing good configuration information (e.g aggregation of server-based applications in data centres);

- enabling people to do their job better (i.e. can people now find CIs?);
- good metrics on 'poor' components should enable better purchasing decisions;
- system and service owners should be identifiable;
- an improved customer perception of the value of IT as a professional partner;
- a recognition of the cost savings through improvements in other processes.

### Selecting KPIs

Delegates suggested concentrating on, say, six simple KPIs that are meaningful to senior management. Don't try to manage too many KPIs. Establishing smart objectives for each stage of improvement was also suggested.

## BOOK CONCLUSION

Chapters 1, 2 and 3 of this book covers the value of a CMS and the challenges faced when implementing configuration management. The practitioners involved in the conference interactive sessions provided feedback on their industry experience and identified practical guidance on what works and what to avoid. The advice in this book will help you to arrive successfully after your organisational and cultural change journey.

By understanding the culture and capability of your organisation today, along with the implementation challenges and risks, you will be better prepared to plan your journey. This will help you to determine your organisation's requirements and develop a clear business case. A good business case should include clear objectives, purpose and scope with the high-level CM requirements for each stakeholder group. Practitioners in the interactive sessions confirmed that adopting best practice programme and project management practices will help you to manage organisational and cultural change.

Both the presenters and practitioners recommend a staged implementation based on industry standards. There are many standards and frameworks that require configuration management, including ITIL, COBIT®, ISO/IEC 20000, ISO/IEC 27001 and CMMI®, as well as the more specific ISO 10007:2003 *Quality management systems – Guidelines for configuration management* and ISO/IEC 19770-1:2006 *Information technology – Software asset management – Part 1, Processes;* and the general standards for software and system lifecycle management, ISO/IEC 12207 and ISO/IEC 15288.

This chapter and Chapter 4 looked at the critical success factors and barriers to implementation. Conference participants identified that most benefits are for the service desk. The service desk, service delivery and operations teams are the most important stakeholder groups that can benefit from a CMS. Many of these teams are daily users of the CMS and they want a CMS to support their daily activities in resolving incidents, problems and managing requests and changes.

Articulating a clear vision for configuration management helps to develop a shared understanding of the benefits across the stakeholder groups. Chapter 8 covered a case study that articulates such a clear CM vision.

The delegates liked the idea that the roles and responsibilities of the CM team should be defined up front, as part of the vision, rather than after tools have been deployed. The approach in Chapter 8 promotes a focus on 'business outcomes' rather than the needs of any particular tool.

Selecting the right scope for an initial implementation can really help to get started. One option that works successfully is to implement configuration management for a business critical service (see Chapter 5). Often a new service or technology provides an opportunity to implement configuration management, for example a technology refresh programme, releasing a new application service or moving into a new data centre.

When getting started, it is important to create a shared understanding of the IT organisation's culture and current capability in delivering solutions and services. Benchmarking your organisation's capability in managing IT and services against industry standards is a useful start. Your starting point will affect the strategy for implementation. At lower levels of organisational and process capability maturity, configuration management supports effective and efficient change management and improved incident and problem management. There is less integration of processes at lower levels of organisational maturity.

The level of maturity also impacts the selection of stakeholder groups. Configuration management often supports release management and deployment of systems and services across the service lifecycle and many stakeholder groups will be involved. The conference identified key stakeholders as the service desk, service delivery and operations teams. If you integrate configuration management with other service management activities there are clearly opportunities to demonstrate added value.

This chapter confirms the useful metrics and key performance indicators that help develop a business case and benefit delivery. Many practitioners seek improvements in business and service performance. Improved performance is enabled by reduced downtime, less incidents, faster times to restore service and higher change success rates. There are also opportunities to improve productivity while reducing costs and risks.

Chapter 6 highlighted the role of measurement, monitoring and control in order to ensure that a system, product, process or service is configured correctly and/or that it functions exactly as specified. Many of the techniques delegates suggested in Chapter 6 are processes that enable detection of configuration, CMS or process failures. Appropriate measures and controls should be defined and monitored across the software, systems and service lifecycle to validate the configuration and to identify improvement opportunities.

Supporting tools and technology enable automation of many IT activities, but it is important to select tools based on a good understanding of the requirements. Practitioners explore the solution options with the different stakeholders to obtain feedback on the feasibility of each option. Chapter 7 outlined a practical approach to defining the requirements for configuration management and a CMS using a top-down approach. Conference participants liked the idea of use case workshops with key stakeholders to define the process requirements and user interactions with the CMS in a structured way.

People and process are key to sharing and maintaining configuration information across the enterprise. Automation and tool support are also an important part of establishing the CMS.

Chapter 9 covered a three-staged approach to tool selection for effective change and configuration management that is recommended by the CMS participant community. Many people involved in tool selection, even those with experience in the process, need to be feel confident that they are following the right path and have the right solution. This is all part of the cultural and organisational change that often needs more focus in implementations.

Bringing the CMS to fruition and populating the CMS are keys aspect of implementation. Chapter 10 dealt with process design and how to identify the definitive data for your CMS that will be used to populate the CMS. It explores the process and data gaps between where you are now and where you want to be with a discussion of the associated practical issues. One key point is the importance of reviewing the process activities with the aim of eliminating steps because this helps to simplify the solution and reduce cost. Chapter 11 covered practical advice on bringing the CMS to fruition with different options for integration of tools and information in the CMS. This chapter covered in-house integration, external systems integration, selecting a primary supplier (vendor) solution and a hybrid approach based on all of all of these.

Throughout the conference, delegates shared their experience of the weak points in their processes for maintaining configuration information, the key inhibitors you may meet in the real world, and some mitigation strategies to deal with them. Many of the issues were similar to the ones covered in this chapter. There was also plenty of practical advice on what works to deliver a CM solution with real benefits.

# APPENDIX
# KEY CONCEPTS AND TERMS

## SYSTEMS, POLICIES, PROCESSES, AND 'JUST DOING IT'

Terminology is a frequent source of confusion in the configuration management space, partly because it is not consistent across the different, rather silo'd, spheres of interest that practitioners occupy. The terminology used in the interactive sessions that form the basis for this book is that used by the configuration management community generally. Other readers my need some explanation of the terms used.

### Just doing it
People at the sharp end (operating or using automated business systems) often say that they just want change managed: 'version control' appears to be enough for them. They want the technology packaged into a version and when Version 2 works (according to some set of criteria) it just replaces Version 1, and business continues.

They often express distrust of written policies and procedures and rely on the skills of trained people in key positions to make change happen successfully, but this is, of course, a policy in itself, albeit one with significant risks attached. It represents an informal and often arbitrary process.

A little thought clarifies the risks of 'just doing it'. Suppose a training course changes what it tells people to do, while existing staff are still doing what they were told to do on the preceding course, or a key person leaves and is replaced by someone with different ideas, or a contractual SLA changes with Version 2, but many operators are still working to the Version 1 SLA. The devil is often in the detail: suppose Version 2 goes live while the training courses and staff desks, chairs, phone system etc. (not included in the technology scope for Version 2) are still only appropriate to the needs of the Version 1 system.

As organisations mature, they usually decide that 'just doing it' is not good enough. As organisations focus on maintaining business continuity as things change, they find that more things, CIs, have to be managed than are within the scope of informal change management processes and application version control. A 'configuration item' is anything that must be managed in order to deliver a service reliably: not just software, but hardware, premises, working environments, people, roles, SLAs and so on.

## Policies and procedures

The first stage in improving things is the adoption of documented configuration management and other policies and procedures, perhaps based on the good practices in ITIL v3.

In the context of this book, formal policies are documented statements of management expectations and intentions and desired good practices, expressed in high-level business terms.

Procedures or practices are the mappings of these onto specific technologies, addressing specific requirements and risks. They represent 'the way in which a thing must be done'.

## Processes

Formal processes are more holistic than procedures. They represent closed-loop systems, with inputs (including human, cultural and organisational inputs), a transformation, and defined outputs contributing to a specific goal. They are usually considered in the context of a framework such as ITIL.

Managing the risk associated with transitioning changed business services into production necessitates formal processes that can be validated, measured and improved. It is important to realise that process is not an end in itself, it is merely a means to an end, the end being a business that can accommodate changes to technology or business processes in a reasonably agile way and continue to deliver business benefit.

An 'institutionalised process' is one that has become part of the operational culture of an organisation. It is easier to follow an institutionalised process than not to follow it, and such processes are available across the whole organisation, wherever they are appropriate. The idea of institutionalising process comes from CMMI® and is associated with increasing organisational maturity.

## Systems

A 'system' is a holistic approach to getting something done, combining people, process and technology with a vision of the desired state. The concept derives from General Systems Theory and the implication is that a system incorporates metrics-based feedback loops to maintain the desired state as the business, its technology and the configuration of its technology changes.

'Systems' and 'processes' therefore overlap considerably. When one is talking in a specific technology context, such as ITIL, one tends to talk about a process; when one is talking at an abstracted business level independent of any particular implementing technologies, one tends to talk about systems.

## Feedback

Feedback is essential to process management, process improvement and holistic systems management.

Figure A1.1 outlines the feedback loop (or monitor control loop) used in ITIL (see Service Operation, Section 5.1, pp. 83–92), which is a typical example of feedback.

A single activity and its output are measured using a predefined norm, or standard, to determine whether it is within an acceptable range of performance or quality. If not, action is taken to rectify the situation or to restore normal performance.

---

**Figure A1.1** The monitor control loop

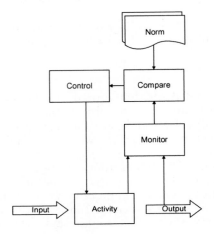

Rectifying any issues may involve critical assessment of either the norms (perhaps they are no longer appropriate to the environment the activity is operating in, or the reasons for lack of compliance, or both).

Monitor control loops can be nested to form complex monitor control loops. For example monitoring and controlling an overall service level for an IT service may require a monitor control loop for the end-to-end service performance that involves the monitoring and control of several process, people, application and infrastructure resources, each with its own monitor control loop.

## A CONSISTENT MODEL FOR THE TERMINOLOGY AROUND CHANGE MANAGEMENT

The ITIL Service Transition volume provides a consistent picture of the processes in Service Transition in Chapter 4. It discusses the place of Change Management in ITIL Service Transition, Section 4.2.

In ITIL Service Transition, Section 4.3, entitled Service Asset and Configuration Management, and overviewed in Chapter 1 of this book, it places asset and CM activities in context to management and planning, controls, verification and risk.

It goes on to place all this in the context of Release and Deployment Management in ITIL Service Transition, Section 4.4.

Readers are advised to read ITIL Service Transition, Chapter 4, in order to make sense of the various terms used when talking about configuration management and place them in context. However, readers from other backgrounds will need to map these terms onto those relevant to their particular context. This is inconvenient, but it is not a serious issue, as long as usage is consistent.
This book uses terms in the ITIL sense (see the Glossary on page xiv).

# NOTES

1 Thanks to Linda Newsom-Ray and Tom Brett (CMSG Conference & Exhibition 24 & 25 June 2003); John Mitchell PhD, MBA, CEng, CITP, FBCS, MBCS, FIIA, MIIA, CISA, QiCA, CFE Managing Director, LHS; Business Control, Editor BCS IRMA Journal: Joint meeting between The CMSG And Information Risk Management & Audit (IRMA) specialist groups July 2007 for the examples this picture is based on.

2 BCS CMSG Conference 2005: Glenn Ellis, Configuration Manager, ADI Limited (Australia).

3 Implementation Stories – Change, Configuration and Release Management 3 October 2001 Nick Hawkins, Telelogic.

4 Linda Newsom-Ray and Tom Brett (CMSG Conference & Exhibition 24 & 25 June 2003).

# INDEX

140

Lightning Source UK Ltd.
Milton Keynes UK
UKOW011825270613

212920UK00011B/628/P